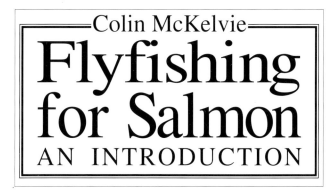

Colin McKelvie

Flyfishing for Salmon

AN INTRODUCTION

Success on 1st January! Two of the earliest possible springers, caught on New Year's Day by two brothers-in-law, on Ireland's River Drowes, where salmon abound and costs are low.

Colin McKelvie

Flyfishing for Salmon

AN INTRODUCTION

SWAN·HILL
PRESS

First published in the UK in 1995
by Swan Hill Press an imprint of Airlife Publishing Ltd

British Library Cataloguing in Publication Data
    A catalogue record for this book
    is available from the British Library

ISBN 1 85310 332 2

Typeset by Litho Link Ltd, Welshpool, Powys
Printed by Butler & Tanner Ltd, Frome and London

Airlife Publishing Ltd
101 Longden Road, Shrewsbury SY3 9EB

For George John Smith
(born 1995)
in hopes that he, too, may one day catch a salmon

Acknowledgements

It is difficult to know where to begin, in trying adequately to acknowledge the help and encouragement of others in the preparation and writing of this book. But its earliest origins lie in the gift of a fishing rod when I was a little boy, and for that I cannot forget the generosity and encouragement of the late Rev. Canon J. I. Lea of Donegal, who started my fishing career when I was barely seven years old.

The intervening thirty-eight years have been marked by so much generous sporting hospitality on salmon rivers, lochs and loughs in every corner of Britain and Ireland that it is simply impossible to thank each of my hosts individually here. But it is to them that I owe gratitude for so many varied opportunities of sport with salmon, on everything from little spate streams to mighty east coast rivers, from sequestered highland lochs to the wild stillwater salmon fisheries of the west of Ireland.

John Buckland, scion of a celebrated angling family and himself an eminent authority on flyfishing for salmon, came quickly and nobly to the rescue with his excellent colour photographs when my own went astray. Ken Walker of Bruce & Walker has taught me more about fishing rod design and performance than anyone else. Chris Donegan of Enniskillen and the staff of the Northern Ireland Tourist Board supplied some important photographs of the salmon fishing scene west of the Irish Sea.

My father and mother patiently endured and quietly encouraged my passion for fishing, sharing the many disappointments and occasional minor triumphs of the early days. Several generations of dogs – Gillie, Bonnie, Brora, Vixen and Clogs – have followed happily at my heels, gone rabbitting along innumerable river banks, and shivered in the bottom of boats on countless fishing days. Each outing would have been much less fun without them.

Before we were married, and probably unaware of what lay in store for her, Judy briefly abandoned the important business of her sunbathing to tail a summer salmon for me on the Dee. Since then, she has coped serenely with a husband who not only goes salmon fishing but compounds the deed by shutting himself away in his study and writing about it as well.

Colin McKelvie
Dumfriesshire
June 1995

Contents

Salmon in lochs provide superb sport. Rivers are not the only haunts of salmon and salmon fishers!

Chapter 1   Why Flyfishing?

Why only flyfishing? After all, salmon can be caught on spun and trolled lures, and are also frequently taken on natural baits such as worm, shrimp and prawn. Also, by their character, many very productive salmon waters simply do not lend themselves to flyfishing, and are rarely fished other than by spinning or bait-fishing. And even the finest beats on Dee, Spey and Tweed are fairly regularly fished by spinning, usually in high water conditions.

The decision to confine this book to flyfishing for salmon stems from my belief, which I think I probably share with most other British and European game fishermen, that it is always more interesting and more satisfying to fish with a fly, and to play and land salmon on fly tackle; and that fly tactics are often as effective as, if not much better than, other sporting rod-and-line methods. To cast a good line with a fly rod is a pleasing activity in itself, and in the course of a long salmon fishing day – or a long salmon fishing career – even the most skilled and lucky fisher will spend a lot more time in casting than in playing fish. If each cast gives the pleasureable sensation of a physical action well executed, even a fishless day can pass very agreeably.

To fish with a fly, and to play and land salmon on fly tackle, is the most interesting and satisfying of all rod-and-line techniques.

Not even the most dedicated spinner of lures or fisher of natural baits would claim that. And the full repertoire of flyfishing tackle and techniques allows the salmon fisher to approach virtually any salmon-holding water with at least a fair chance of success, in all but the most extreme conditions. Even in the lowest water or the deepest pools, the strongest currents or the slackest dubs, the coldest snow-melt water or the warmest waters of high summer, and in all but the most coloured floods, a correctly-fished fly can take salmon – yes, even in the brackish water of a sea-pool.

This book's commitment to flyfishing does not stem from any purist distaste for spinning or bait fishing – I have done plenty of both, and will continue to do so – but from my conviction that every salmon caught on fly tackle will yield the maximum pleasure and excitement to its captor, and that modern flyfishing encompasses a vast range of techniques and tactics which make it uniquely adaptable to the successful sporting pursuit of salmon under almost all conditions.

Another aim of this book is to dispel some of the unnecessary mystique which appears to surround flyfishing for salmon. There is a special magic about salmon and salmon fishing, and therein lies much of its unique appeal. But too many would-be salmon fishers, including many who are already very competent and successful fly fishers for trout, are intimidated by the aura of exclusivity which they associate with salmon fishing. Too often it conjures up images of private waters on landed estates, of retinues of gillies and boatmen clad in smart estate tweeds, of the rich and privileged at play on estates where ordinary mortals never tread. This image is not only incorrect; it is downright dangerous for the public per-ception of game fishing in particular and field sports in general because it is only partly true. It is further compounded by periodic press reports of salmon fishings selling for millions, of one-week timeshare units changing hands at tens of thousands of pounds, and of the oft-quoted statistic that the average fishing visitor to Scotland will spend something like £600-£800 for each salmon he catches. Such figures have some basis in fact, but they combine to give the erroneous impression that all worthwhile salmon fishing is available only to those with vast funds at their disposal, or with powerful connections and privileged friends.

In fact, salmon fishing is a much more democratic and accessible activity than that, and always has been. For every Rod fishing a private beat as a high-paying tenant or a privileged guest there will be at least one or two others on the same river, fishing readily accessible waters controlled by a local angling association or club, or with a daily or weekly ticket from a hotel or estate. On the less fashionable rivers in the west of Scotland, and especially in Ireland, there may be virtually no "smart" salmon fishers at all. If we subtracted the total annual salmon catch with rod and line on such accessible "ordinary" waters from the total national rod catch we would see a vast difference; and I would guess with some confidence that well over half of all rod-caught salmon on British and Irish waters fall to fishers on relatively inexpensive association, club or "public" waters.

Nevertheless, it would be misleading to imply that ample funds and good personal contacts do not greatly help the salmon fisher's catch rate. Access to the most productive beats of classic rivers at peak times of the season is highly sought after, and the demand vastly outstrips the supply, simply because so many fish are consistently caught on these special stretches of river. The basic economic laws of supply and demand therefore dictate that rents are very high, and those who rent prime fishing weeks tend to renew their tenancies from year to year, thereby creating long waiting lists and a "dead men's shoes" system of acquiring the tenancy of certain beats on certain rivers. If you want to fish the Kelso beats of Tweed in the autumn, or the fabled waters of the Grimersta in summer, or the Upper Brora or the Helmsdale in spring, or the massive rivers of Norway and north-west Russia at any time, you should be prepared to pay hundreds and sometimes thousands of pounds to do so, and even then you may have to wait some years for a vacancy to occur. Or else you should cultivate the friendship of one of the existing tenants! Salmon fishing throughout Britain and Europe is so thoroughly exploited and so eagerly sought after that there is a definite correlation between the amount of money you pay and the prospects of catching lots of fish. Indeed, there are prime, high-priced beats on some British and Irish rivers where a total novice, under the tutelage of a good gillie and at a choice time of the season, will be extremely unlucky not to

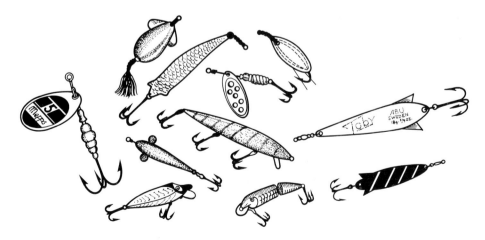

A fly, well chosen and correctly fished, can hold its own with lures and baits under most conditions.

catch at least one or two fish, and where a more skilful and experienced fisher may take a very heavy basket.

But just because you cannot afford the very finest beats, do not despair of catching salmon. To do this would be as foolish as to give up shooting because you can't afford to rent the very best grouse moors, or to abandon yachting because you can't afford to keep an ocean racer moored at Cowes. There is still plenty of really excellent salmon fishing which is well within the average person's budget. And, as with many other sports, the salmon flyfisher's success will tend to be in direct proportion to the skills he develops, the persistence he displays, and the care and concentration with which he undertakes his fishing.

For all these reasons, it seems sensible to provide an outline of the sport of salmon fishing with a fly, intended principally for the newcomer who has had some experience of flyfishing for trout, and who would now like to to venture into the exciting but sometimes daunting world of salmon flyfishing, an accessible activity that is all too often obscured and made to seem unapproachable by a combination of mystique and myth and an aura of intimidating exclusivity. The future of a wonderful sport and the fate of a magnificent sporting species are far too important to be left only in the hands of an inner circle of afficionados.

Chapter 2   The Quarry –
Salmo salar

The Atlantic salmon is a familiar fish, even to non-fishers. Who has not eaten its delicious flesh in some form, cold or hot, fresh or smoked, tinned or fresh from the river? It has been widely used in a thousand-and-one images, in art and as an advertising symbol, to proclaim not only its food value and its sporting appeal but also the way it symbolises supremely wild elegance. The wild Atlantic salmon, that leaping bar of shimmering delight, is a metaphor for all the unfettered wildness and natural energy that is so lacking in an increasingly mechanised and urbanised world.

Salmo salar – the leaping Atlantic salmon – surging back to spawn in its native river.

It belongs to a distinct genus – *Salmo* – in the great scheme of fishes, as classified by taxonomists; and its second Latin name – *salar* – is definitive. This is "Salmo the leaper", the fish which flings itself with unrivalled power and determined energy upwards and over the obstacles in its path as it returns from the sea to the freshwater streams where its life began, and where in turn it will mate and spawn and reproduce a new generation of its kind.

The genus *Salmo* and the family of the Salmonidae also embrace the indigenous trout of the British Isles, the sedentary brown trout of rivers and lakes and also the wandering migrant seatrout, and it is not entirely unknown for salmon and seatrout to hybridise in the wild. Other distantly related kinds of fish also claim the vernacular name of salmon, and probably the best known of these are the five species of so-called Pacific salmon, which belong to the genus *Oncorhynchus*, and are best known for their prodigious spawning runs up the rivers of western Canada and the United States. (A sixth species, *O. masou*, is found only in Japan.) The salmon which are so familiar to the sporting fishermen and netsmen of the Pacific seaboard of Canada and the United States are best known as chum, coho, pink, sockeye and chinook salmon, all are *Oncorhynchus* species, and apart from some obvious differences in their appearance and anatomy, these Pacific salmon share one interesting and dramatic characteristic – all spawn once only and then die. In this they differ from the Atlantic salmon,

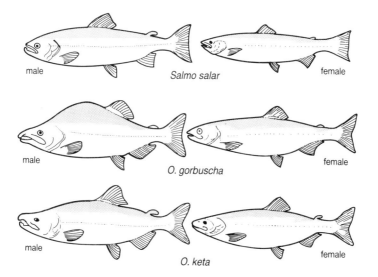

Atlantic and Pacific salmon species. The Atlantic salmon is unique to the rivers of the North Atlantic basin.

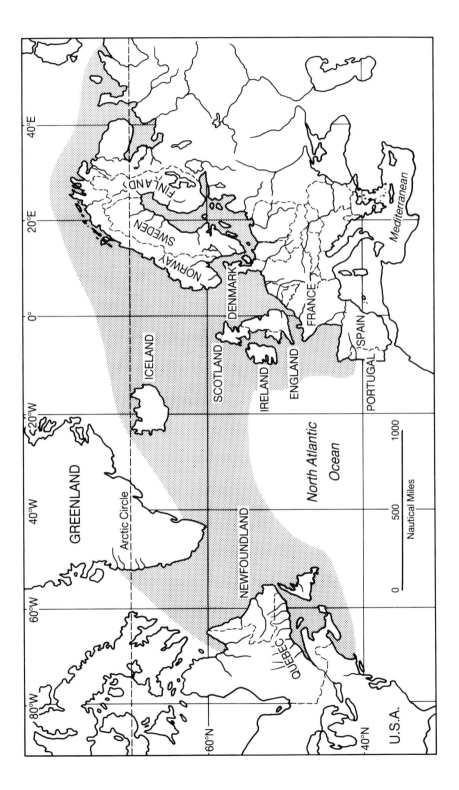

The range of the Atlantic salmon in Europe and North America

and from its close cousins the seatrout and the brown trout, all of which are capable of spawning and surviving to do so again, perhaps several times. Research has indicated that about 60 per cent of Atlantic salmon do not survive their first spawning, and only a small proportion of those that manage to drop downstream to the sea after spawning succeed in recovering condition and avoiding predators to return and spawn a second time. Third and fourth time spawners, while not unknown, are very rare. Nevertheless, this capacity for survival and recovery to return for a second spawning constitutes a definitive distinction between the life of the Atlantic salmon of Europe and the eastern rivers of North America and the *Oncorynchus* species of the Pacific rivers of North America and eastern Asia.

The life cycle of the Atlantic salmon, the species with which this book is solely concerned, is best considered as beginning with the return of mature and sexually active adult fish from a period of life at sea to spawn in fresh water. Salmon occur in every suitable river and stream around the North Atlantic Basin, from the sub-Arctic waters of Iceland, Norway, Canada and north-west Russia to as far south as the lower latitudes of Spain and Portugal. Even countries with no Atlantic or Baltic coastline, including Switzerland, Luxembourg and Czechoslovakia, used to have big runs of salmon, which travelled hundreds of miles upstream in the rivers Rhine and Vltava, for thousands of years between the end of the last Ice Age and the coming of recent barrages and pollution which have now destroyed these salmon populations.

Salmon ascend from the sea into freshwater, impelled upstream by an overwhelmingly powerful urge to revisit the waters where their own lives began as fertilised eggs, and where they first lived and developed as fry and parr. There they mate and spawn, and leave a cache of fertilised eggs which will develop into alevins, fry, parr and migrant smolts. These seagoing migrants will grow fast on the rich marine food supply until, after a total of five or six years have passed since they hatched from the egg, they represent a new generation of grilse and mature salmon, another spawning run to begin the wonderful cycle all over again.

Salmon move inshore and run upstream into freshwater for one purpose only – spawning. This is the sole reason why they forsake the boundless saline environment of the ocean, with its rich feeding, for the claustrophobic confines of rivers, lochs and streams which are generally acidic, in which they do not feed much if at all, and where the majority of them will die after mating and spawning.

But salmon run at many different times of the year. Indeed, they are known to run up British and Irish rivers in every month of the year, and in one or two of the largest river systems such as the Tweed and the Tay a certain number of fresh salmon probably enter the river in every single

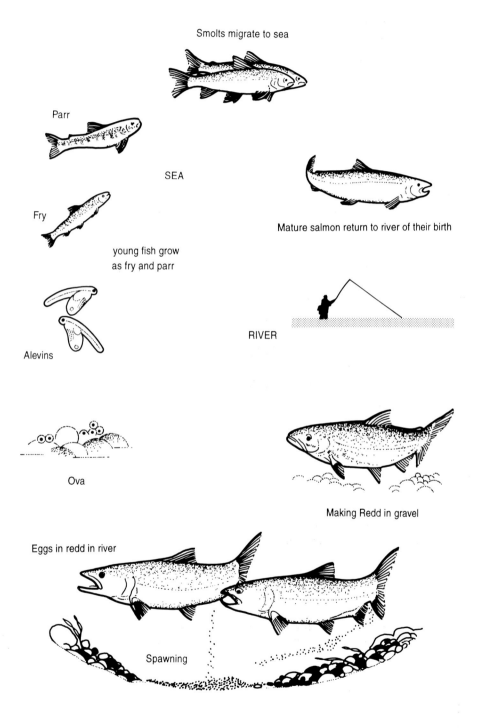

Smolts migrate to sea

Parr

SEA

Fry

Mature salmon return to river of their birth

young fish grow
as fry and parr

Alevins

RIVER

Ova

Making Redd in gravel

Eggs in redd in river

Spawning

The salmon's life cycle from egg to mature spawning adult.

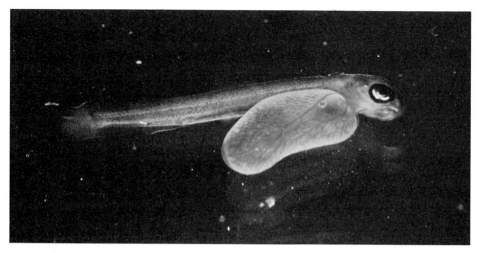

A recently-hatched salmon alevin, showing the prominent yolk sac that provides it with nourishment.

A salmon parr in the gravelly shallows of the river's nursery areas. Note the distinctive 'fingerprint' parr marks on its flanks.

week throughout the year. (And the dedicated salmon fisherman can, if he wishes, legally fish with rod and line for salmon at some stage in every month of the year, with several Irish and Scottish rivers offering good fishing from 1st January and some rivers in Cornwall permitting fishing until well into December.)

By tradition, sporting fishermen and commercial netsmen refer to runs of fresh salmon in association with the four seasons of the year: so-called spring salmon are allocated to any time between 1st January and the end of May. Summer fish, often smallish grilse which have spent barely one year at sea, belong to the months of June, July and August. The autumn run, increasingly important in most British Isles rivers and usually comprising fish which are sizeable, sexually well developed and ready to spawn, arrive from September until the end of November.

That leaves "winter salmon", which are seldom referred to in fishing literature, and which usually represent those fish which enter a river during the angling close season, after the end of one fishing season and the opening of another. These may be either very ripe spawning fish, in which case they will probably make a headlong upstream dash for their spawning grounds, or very early springers, silvery bright and not yet in a sufficiently advanced physical condition to spawn, which may linger in freshwater for perhaps a further eleven months before they finally spawn. Winter-run salmon are not uncommon in some rivers, including the Annan and the Nith in south-west Scotland, which often receive large runs of mature spawners after the close of angling in mid or late November, and in Irish rivers such as the Drowes, where bright, so-called spring fish regularly begin running in December, well before the January 1st opening day of the fishing season and almost a full year before they will eventually spawn in the headwater streams far inland.

Most individual British Isles salmon rivers tend to be particularly known for the runs of fish they receive at certain times of the year. After all, those are the times when they attract the fisherman's particular interest. The Hampshire Avon, for example, still retains something of its earlier reputation for some massive spring salmon, and the Aberdeenshire Dee, the Helmsdale and the Brora in Sutherland are also known for good runs of smaller but silvery bright fish in the earliest and coldest months of the year. Except in very dry summers, small summer salmon and grilse appear in the majority of Britain's northern and western rivers and sea-linked lochs, and since the 1960s the autumn run has increasingly become the mainstay of salmon angling on most rivers, including such classic waters as the Tweed, the Spey and the Nith. These patterns are inevitably reflected in the availability and costs of good fishing beats at these productive times of the year, and the tenancy of a prime autumn beat on Tweed or a March week on the Helmsdale will probably demand not only a generous budget but also a measure of patience. It may take years on the waiting list before you inherit dead men's shoes on such highly desirable waters.

A rod-caught salmon is always a fish to be coveted, but in the flyfisher's eyes the glittering spring fish is the most prized of all by far. Bright and silvery-fresh from the sea, perhaps arrived so recently that he still bears the parasitic sea-lice with (in the case of the females) their long tails or egg strings which soon fall off in fresh water, it is in the peak of perfection, a poem of symmetry, elegance, power and wild beauty. The shimmering grilse of late spring and summer have a special charm, and the aggressively marked autumn cock fish in his vermiculated livery and sporting a ferociously hooked kype on his lower jaw is a noble and awesome sight. But the pristine silver ingot of a spring salmon is in a class of its own, the perfect example of a fish in the full splendour of its glorious maturity.

This staggering of the timing of runs of fish through the year is an effective device whereby Nature takes care of her own. Should the ripe, imminent spawners of late autumn meet with some disaster on their homeward run, such as serious predation, a polluted river or the destruction of their spawning areas, the spring run will soon follow, bringing a further batch of fish into the river, where they are at least safe from the hazards of life at sea. Likewise, any natural or man-made misfortune which may strike these spring fish may be offset by a successful spawning by those which follow in the summer months, and in this way Nature avoids putting all her eggs in one basket. Instead she spreads her risk, rather like a wise speculator on the stockmarket, and so the safety of future salmon stocks is not imperilled by everything depending upon the success of a single spawning run.

Salmon are migrants, which spawn in freshwater, which hatch there from the egg and spend the first months and years of their lives in the nursery areas of the stream, first as alevins, then as fry, then as parr and finally as smolts, by which time they will have attained some 4-7 inches in length and be between 15 months and five years of age. Relatively rich waters in mild southern climates, such as the Frome, the Test and the Hampshire Avon, produce smolts which are ready to migrate to sea about 15 months after the eggs hatch, while the young salmon in the cold rivers of western Norway with their low water temperatures and limited food availability may not become smolts until six or seven years have elapsed. In most Scottish and Irish rivers the young fish are ready to migrate at the age of two to four years.

Smoltation is the prelude to a gradual downstream migration, and the young fish develop a silvery body coloration caused by the secretion of a substance called guanin, which blots out the dark fingerprint-like parr markings on the flanks, and imparts an overall silvery brightness. This contrasts with the increasingly dark colour of the little salmon's tail and pectoral fins, and these are the most obvious visible signs of the changes they undergo as a prelude to migration and a new pattern of life at sea. Smolts drop gradually downstream during the months of spring and early summer, and at the river mouth or in the estuary they become acclimatised to the increasingly saltiness of the water. Once they have adjusted to their wholly new saline environment, they will undergo the rapid phase of growth which is promoted by a rich diet of small fish and various sea creatures, and which will boost average weights from 3-4 ounces to as much as 6-7 pounds after a single year at sea. A salmon which returns to freshwater after one year at sea is correctly known as a grilse, while the word salmon should, strictly speaking, be reserved for those fish which have spent a continuous period of two or more sea-winters in the ocean before making their first return to freshwater.

Young salmon are normally insatiably active feeders in rivers during the parr stage of their lives, and few trout or salmon fishers have not had parr repeatedly taking artificial flies intended for their older brothers and cousins. Smolts are even more voracious and indiscriminate in their feeding, developing a vigorous feeding impulse as part of their transform-ation and preparation for migration and subsequent months of feeding at sea.

The salmon's pattern of spawning and early growth in fresh water, followed by massive growth and the achievement of maturity at sea, followed by a return to mate and spawn in fresh water, is what fisheries biologists call an anadromous pattern of life. It is the reverse of the procedure that can be observed in some other species such as eels, which spawn and spend their early lives at sea, returning to grow and spend most of their adult lives in fresh water, before the reproductive impulse drives them downstream and out to spawn at sea again. This reverse pattern of life is known as catadromous behaviour.

The salmon's life at sea still remains something of a mystery, despite intense interest over the centuries and a good deal of research in recent years. Ancient writers like Pliny in the first century AD knew about salmon, and appreciated the mystery of their comings and goings, and early modern naturalists like Conrad Gesner were aware of their upstream migration from the sea into rivers. Isaak Walton, an avid reader of old authors and a ready borrower of their wisdom, knew that salmon come up from the sea and breed in freshwater, but the marine phase of the salmon's life remained unknown to him, and it was a continuing subject for speculation among his contemporaries and later generations. Hector Boethius, in his *History of Scotland*, written in 1517, came closer than most

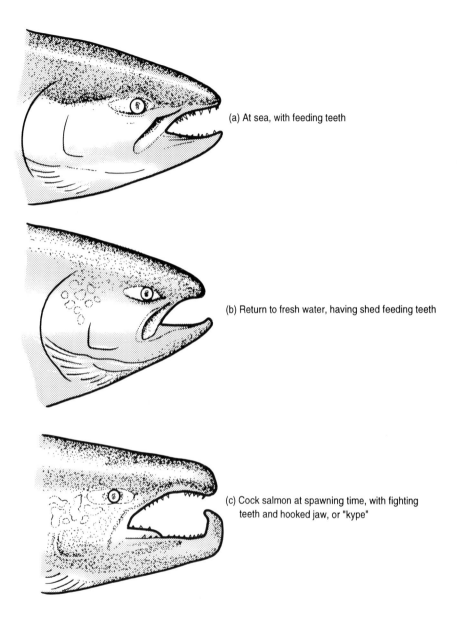

(a) At sea, with feeding teeth

(b) Return to fresh water, having shed feeding teeth

(c) Cock salmon at spawning time, with fighting teeth and hooked jaw, or "kype"

The salmon's teeth: feeding teeth at sea (*top*), toothless and non-feeding on return to fresh water (*middle*), and with fighting teeth and hooked jaw kype at spawning time (*bottom*).

to the truth in his account of salmon running upriver in summer, with fry and smolts to be seen in the spring. "From henceforth they go to sea, where within the space of 20 days they grow to a marvellous greatness, and then returning again toward the place of generation, they show a notable spectacle not unworthy to be considered . . ." Poor Boethius! The very idea of a salmon surging from infancy to maturity in just 20 days at sea seems comical to us now, but he had made a simple mistake, not realising that the well grown returning grilse and salmon of summer were not the smolts he had seen descending in spring, but the migrants of a year or two earlier. Three centuries later, in 1828, Sir Humphry Davy held an opinion not much different, stating that salmon "migrate to the sea in spring and run up the rivers of all sizes in summer and autumn". Grilse he defined as "a young salmon, of the earliest born this spring".

Voracious feeders at sea, where they put on such weight and vigour, salmon undergo a sudden and total cessation of feeding when they re-enter freshwater. They lose their marine-phase feeding teeth and their appetite and digestive processes are suppressed. Once back in freshwater they will go for many months without feeding, perhaps almost a year in the case of fish which run upstream in December and January but do not spawn until the following October or November, which is an indication of how long these fish are capable of living off their accumulated reserves of condition while still retaining the energy necessary to endure the rigours of spawning. As spawning approaches the cock fish grow a fresh set of teeth, which are designed this time not for feeding but for aggression and fighting, as rival males meet and confront one another on the gravelly spawning reaches of the headwaters. With its impressive teeth, vivid vermiculated coloration and the hooked kype of its lower jaw, a cock salmon in prime spawning condition is a sight to inspire awe and respect.

The suppression of the feeding instinct of salmon in freshwater has an obvious explanation, and makes perfect sense for biological reasons. Mature salmon are big, voracious fish at sea, and if they were to continue to feed in freshwater their prey would be their own younger cousins, the smolts and parr and fry that are the main residents of the rivers. A big influx of hungry salmon into the freshwater habitat of the river would quickly devour and destroy all the young salmon and trout, which would scarcely be conducive to the perpetuation of these species. The fasting of the salmon is an adaptation for preserving the younger and smaller fish from attack, and for eliminating any possible competition for food in the river or loch, which is infinitely less food-rich than the off-shore and high-seas regions from which the mature fish have just returned. Back in freshwater for the sole purpose of eventual mating and spawning, the adult salmon "live off their hump", drawing on the massive reserves of weight that they accumulated while far off at sea. A fish that re-enters freshwater eight or nine months prior to spawning may lose almost one-third of its weight during that time – another reason why the fresh springer is the angler's supreme prize, for it is then in the full plumpness and vigour of its maturity, and at its peak in terms of coloration and elegance of form.

The non-feeding behaviour of all salmon in freshwater is the great conundrum and challenge for all rod and line fishermen. How do we induce a fish that is not disposed to feed to take any interest in our lures and baits and flies? No book can entirely unlock that enduring mystery, but the whole art and craft of the salmon flyfisher is addressed to achieving the seemingly impossible – persuading a salmon to take a lure into its mouth at a period in its life cycle when its natural disposition is not to feed at all.

Why salmon take a lure or bait is a topic that has devoured acres of paper in countless books and angling magazines over many generations, and the salmon's taking of the lure has been variously attributed to motives of curiosity, aggression, playfulness or a momentary triggering of the normally suppressed feeding instinct. Sometimes it may be a combination of two or more of these factors, but the puzzle remains unresolved until the scientists' researches can get to the root of the matter. But the real answer, however fascinating, will rob all angling for salmon of much of its particular mystique. After all, what sporting fisherman genuinely wants to have a fly or lure that never, ever fails? Uncertainty and surprise, expectancy and disappointment are of the very essence of salmon fishing, with fly or by any other method.

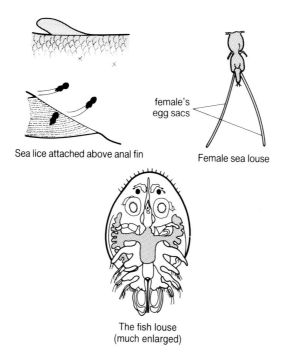

Sea lice attached above anal fin

female's egg sacs

Female sea louse

The fish louse
(much enlarged)

The presence of sea lice indicates a fresh-run fish recently up from the sea. The female parasite's 'tails' – actually egg sacs – drop off first in freshwater.

Long generations of empirical observation by salmon anglers has produced overwhelming evidence that a fresh fish, just into the river on one of the most recent tides, is the likeliest to be a free taker of the fly – and any other lure or bait, for that matter. It seems fair to assume that such a salmon, just hours or even minutes away from saltwater, may still retain something of its former impulse to feed, and that a lure bearing some resemblance to its accustomed marine prey will be taken as a feeding act. And if aggression and curiosity are also likely motives, it also seems probable that these will be to the fore at this critical period. After all, here is a mature fish that has returned to water that it last saw as a diminitive smolt a year or two ago, and which is undergoing the major stresses of adapting its metabolism to the shock of a new freshwater environment after long months at sea. Is such a fish not likely to be nervy, alert and on edge in its unfamiliar new surroundings?

If the suppression of the fish's appetite is the general rule in freshwater, there are nevertheless important exceptions to that rule. Why else would worming be such an effective method of catching salmon? A prawn or a shrimp, or a fly imitating one or other of them, might be seized out of anger or curiosity, but a bundle of lobworms ledgered on the bottom of a pool would appear to offer no such excitement. The success of the worm seems to be a clear pointer to the conclusion that some salmon do sometimes attempt to feed in freshwater. And even if the typical pre-spawning fish is not to be tempted to take any lure or bait, the post-spawner recovers its appetite very quickly and becomes a ready taker of lures of all kinds. Kelts are notorious for their eagerness to grab at the flies and spun lures of the early-season angler.

There are certain signs that denote a salmon freshly in from the sea, compared to one that has been in freshwater for some time. First and most obvious, often long before the fish is in the net or on the bank, is the wonderful shimmering silver of its coloration. This is a magical hue that is difficult to describe adequately. It is not the hard and rather one-dimensional metallic sheen of a kelt, but an infinitely subtle silver that gleams with hints and layers of rare blues and rose pinks, an almost opalescent quality which is the crowning glory of a fresh-run salmon.

Its head and jaws appear small and trim by comparison with the heaviness and kypiness that develop in late summer and autumn, after many weeks or months of freshwater residence, and the edges of its fins and tail will be crisp and sharp compared to the more ragged outline of staler salmon. This perfection of fin and tail is the mark of the truly wild salmon, and contrasts sharply with the rounded, stunted fins and tail of a salmon that is a fish-farm escapee. Within the confines of a hatchery unit and later a sea-cage, the latter's fin and tail development are inhibited by its confinement and crowding, unlike the boundless freedom of a wild fish at liberty in the ocean. A great many British and Irish rivers, especially spatey rivers on western coasts, receive sudden and unwelcome runs of farmed escapees from cages moored in saltwater lochs and sheltered coves, often as a consequence of storm damage to the cages. In addition to their leaden and uninspiring qualities as sporting fish, these farmed specimens are also unwelcome because of the threat they may pose to the genetic integrity of the indigenous wild salmon population.

The sign that puts the unimpeachable seal of authenticity on a fresh-run wild salmon is the presence of sea-lice, small parasites that the adult fish has acquired in the sea, and which quickly atrophy and fall off the host after it has spent a little time in freshwater. These small parasites, only four millimetres or so across, look like flattened olive-hued versions of the little ticks that are commonly found on dogs and sheep and deer, and they tend to be sited particularly in the rear section of the salmon's body, especially around the anal and ventral fins, and along the fish's back. The presence of even one or two sea lice can be taken as proof that the fish has not been in the river for more than four or five days at most, and if there is a large number of them there is a reasonable presumption that the fish is fresher still. Female sea lice can be distinguished by their long opaque tails or strings, which are their egg clusters, and these tails drop off within a matter of hours exposure to freshwater. The presence of what are often referred to as long-tailed sea lice – i.e. females with egg clusters – is therefore a highly prized indication that the host fish is only a few hours away from the sea – the salmon angler's greatest prize of all.

The disappearance of its sea lice is only the first of the visible changes that appear in salmon after they return to freshwater. Gradually the breathtaking freshness of its first silver gives way to a progressive darkening of coloration, and a fish that has been in the river for a month or so will have begun to exhibit a slight darkening of its flanks as a hint of brown hues begins to become apparent, and this darkening continues until the transformation is complete, most obviously in the form of the rich coloration and vermiculation that are so apparent in a cock salmon that is close to spawning. The hen salmon darkens too, but not to the same dramatic extent as her mate, and her head remains altogether neater in shape than the powerfully heavy and aggressively hooked jowls and kype of a cock salmon in spawning fettle.

"Kippery" is a common term for the characteristic reddish-russet of a salmon close to spawning, especially the cock fish, and these are often so strikingly different in colour and conformation from the shimmering springer that a casual observer might doubt that they were the same creature. By tradition, and by law, late season hen fish that are heavy with eggs are returned to the water, and there are hefty penalties for the taking of what are formally known as "unseasonable fish", irrespective of whether the statutory fishing season is open or not. A reddish cock fish may be well worth keeping, and most of these are sent for smoking, which is a much preferable option to cooking them fresh; but a very coloured cock fish full of milt is clearly an unseasonable fish and should be returned to the water. Apart from any legal consideration, this is a sensible conservation measure.

The gravid hen salmon is an especially valuable creature, for she holds within her thousands of eggs that will shortly be shed into the trough or redd the fish excavates in the rough river gravels, there to be fertilised by her mate. A cock fish that falls by the wayside, whether to a netsman, a poacher, an otter or a rod angler, is only one less possible source of the milt that is vital to fertilise those eggs. One cock salmon lost may readily be replaced by another, but a gravid hen that is lost almost certainly represents a net loss to the spawning total of that river in that season. So solicitous is Nature about the future of the species, and so anxious is she that the females' eggs should be fertilised, that even the little male parr that are still growing in the river are sexually precocious to the point of being able to fertilise the eggs of an adult female salmon that weighs perhaps forty or sixty times more than himself.

Nature's many careful provisions for the welfare of the salmon – abundant food during its life at sea, the seasonal staggering of the return runs to reduce the likelihood of pre-spawning losses, and the mechanism whereby male parr can fertilise mature females' eggs – seem especially poignant when we consider the ruthless ways in which man has over-exploited the Atlantic salmon in the last decades of this century.

In the nineteenth and early twentieth centuries most sportsmen and fisheries experts agreed that salmon fed far out at sea, probably for periods of one or two years; but exactly where the salmon went to feed at sea remained largely unknown until the late 1950s. That mystery was a huge blessing to the welfare of salmon at sea, for man can only exploit a species if he can first find it, and salmon simply seemed to vanish into the vastness of the Atlantic, not to be seen again until they returned through the estuaries and the sea-pools. In the 66-year period prior to 1954 only 78 salmon had been recorded as caught at sea off Scotland, an astonishingly small total for a period covering two-thirds of a century and in heavily fished waters around the hugely productive salmon rivers of Scotland.

Then in 1956 an event occurred which was to become a milestone in the history of man's understanding of the movements of salmon at sea and his subsequent ability to exploit them by commercial fishing on the high seas. A salmon which had been tagged as a post-spawner (i.e. a kelt) in a Scottish river was caught off the west coast of Greenland, the first indication that this region of the north-west Atlantic is an important feeding ground for salmon. Further tagged salmon from Canadian, Swedish, British, French and Irish rivers were caught in the same sea area in the late 1950s, and the seas off west Greenland and in the Davis Strait area soon became the hunting ground of commercial vessels using drift nets specifically in search of high seas salmon. The newly developed synthetic monofilament netting was cheap, light and deadly effective, and a single vessel could tow as much as 20 miles of drifting net behind it. The high seas catches of salmon were vast as an international free-for-all began, and this massive harvest was taken from fish which had migrated from many countries on both sides of the North Atlantic. Perhaps the grimmest dimension of this wholesale netting was to be seen in the fact that much of this harvest of salmon was being taken by fishing vessels from nations which had no indigenous salmon stocks, whose waters contributed nothing to the sea-going population of salmon, and which made no attempts to promote the species' future welfare. Commercial fishermen from Britain and Norway, for example, were at least able partially to excuse themselves by claiming that they were harvesting a species that originated in their carefully conserved home rivers. Boats from home ports in salmonless nations could make no such claims, and were seen as simply quarrying at a rich natural resource which they were unable and unwilling to make sustainable by conservation measures or restraint in fishing pressure. Above all, the Faeroese commercial fishers attracted first concern and then hostility and widespread denunciation for

A salmon kelt. The head appears large in relation to the wasted thinness of the body. There is a harsh metallic sheen, frayed fins and tail, and the gills are infested with maggots.

their vast catches of salmon that "belonged" to countries with salmon-producing freshwater systems.

Such was the pressure of high seas fishing on sea-going salmon in the 1960s and 1970s that it quickly constituted a major threat to the very survival of the species in the rivers of the Atlantic basin. Since the 1980s, however, a network of international organisations and a succession of treaties has exercised a restraining influence on the worst excesses of exploitation at sea, while some of the most destructive high seas netting operations, notably that operated from the Faeroes, have been bought out and shut down. The market demand for fresh salmon has always been high and has massively increased in the postwar period, but the bulk of this demand is now being met by sales of intensively farmed salmon grown in cages on a commercial basis, in the sheltered lochs of western Scotland and the fjords of Norway. Salmon farming has undoubtedly relieved much of the netting pressure on wild salmon stocks at a time when the fortunes of the wild Atlantic salmon were becoming extremely precarious and its very survival was threatened. Throughout the rivers of Britain and Ireland, the numbers of returning salmon are (1994) barely more than 25%-30% of their average levels in the early 1960s, despite the controls on high seas fishing and the reduced inshore and estuary netting pressures that have resulted from the buying-out and closure of many netting operations.

In the mid 1990s the most significant and destructive salmon netting operations that remain in the eastern Atlantic are the (mainly illegal) offshore drift netting off the western coast of Ireland, and the licensed but highly controversial drift net fishery in the North Sea, off the Northumberland coast. Both operations continue to intercept large numbers of mature salmon on their return migrations towards the British and Irish rivers of their birth. Illegal drift netting with monofilament nets of unlawfully small mesh size not only take many mature salmon, but also destroy large numbers of small grilse and seatrout that would normally escape, and the evidence can plainly been seen when even quite small seatrout of 1-1½ lbs are seen to exhibit severe net-marking.

The effects of these recent and continuing threats to salmon on the high seas have been compounded by changes in the freshwater habitats of their natal rivers. Pollution and water abstraction have caused rivers in southern Britain to suffer from dirtier water quality and much reduced rates of water flow, both of which have caused serious deterioration of the salmon's freshwater habitat, especially in the spawning and nursery areas where the mature fish spawn and the growing fry and parr develop. The salmon populations of rivers such as the Avon and the Test in Hampshire are now a mere fraction of their size in the 1960s. Northern and western Britain and Ireland have undergone critical changes in land use, of which the most notable and destructive for salmon has been the epidemic spread of blanket conifer afforestation. Ancient and natural drainage patterns in the headwaters of river catchments have been replaced by new systems of upland and forestry drainage, which causes much accelerated run-off of surface water, causing sudden and violent spates followed by an equally abrupt fall-off in water levels. Disturbance and siltation of vital spawning and nursery areas have resulted in many such rivers. In addition to these wild fluctuations in water levels, conifers catch and retain acidity originating from industrial pollution and the burning of fossil fuels that is precipitated in the form of rain and snow – the much-publicised phenomenon of acid rain – and this damaging acidity finds its way into the water-courses, often accompanied by flushes of dangerous heavy metals, notably aluminium. Increased acidity in upland rivers that are already naturally somewhat acidic in character militates against insect and invertebrate life in the water, thereby reducing the food supply available to salmon and trout parr in the nursery areas, while high aluminium levels cause deformities and illness in the young fish, and often prove fatal. The problem is especially acute in rivers that flow over granite and similar underlying rocks, that are acidic by nature and can offer no buffering to offset influxes of acidity, such as can occur where rivers flow over limestone and chalk. Granite is the predominant bedrock of many of the most celebrated salmon river systems of Scotland and Ireland. In these and other ways, the Atlantic salmon is under serious threat both in its freshwater habitats and during its times of migration and feeding far out at sea.

Happily, every salmon-producing country around the north Atlantic has finally responded to the proddings of conservationists, fisheries biologists and anglers with important research and practical conservation measures, much of which is funded by the voluntary donations of the rod-fishing community, who have an urgent desire to secure the future wellbeing of their most highly prized and best loved game fish.

The outlook is not all doom and gloom for the salmon and the salmon fisher: there would be no point in writing a book for the newcomer to salmon fishing if that were so. Increasingly, there are heartening signs that the salmon's true value as a sporting asset and as a magnificent member of our freshwater fauna is being recognised, after generations of having been taken too much for granted, and after the dark days of the 1970s and early 1980s, when the carelessness and greed of one generation brought its populations close to the verge of extinction. Conservationists and ecologists see a thriving salmon population as a living barometer that provides evidence of the purity and healthiness of a river catchment, while the importance of the salmon as an economic asset to the remoter parts of northern and western Britain provides a powerful incentive to ensure that there should be fish for the salmon fisherman to catch with rod and line. Farmed salmon now supply the bulk of the demand from restaurants and supermarkets, leaving the wild stocks to be managed as a sustainable resource from which the sporting fisherman can take a modest annual harvest, and in doing so make a substantial contribution to the economies of regions that often have few natural assets to generate wealth. The salmon fishers and their families spend money in the hotels, the gift shops, the pubs, the petrol stations, in addition to what they spend directly on fishing and tackle and gillies' wages. There is plenty of hard-nosed common sense, or cynical self-interest, if you wish to call it that – the practical effects are the same – in keeping the wild salmon as a flourishing resource to draw the fishers and their companions back each season, quite apart from the ethical and aesthetic arguments for maintaining rivers full of wild and beautiful fish.

Never before has the wild Atlantic salmon been so highly prized and accorded such profound respect and widespread publicity. Earlier generations of salmon fishers may have enjoyed their golden ages, when salmon abounded and rod catches were large and frequent, but the 1990s and beyond offer a new prospect of continuing sport in a climate of well-informed fisheries management. Today's angler works hard for his few fish and prizes them accordingly; and never before has the fishing community been ready to put so much eager committment and funds into the vital work of conservation and fisheries improvement.

Chapter 3   The Costs of Salmon Fishing

It is quite possible to pay £5000 and even more for a single week's salmon fishing for one Rod. But it is equally possible to find an enjoyable and productive stretch of salmon river which you can fish for £30 a week. There is even some absolutely free salmon fishing to be had. The estuaries of most rivers are entirely accessible, and it is not unknown for salmon to be caught in brackish and saltwater.

Even the very finest rivers of Grampian and the Borders can occasionally yield a good day at modest cost. Tackle shops and fishing hotels by the Dee, the Spey and Tweed often hear of an unexpected day going begging, perhaps when a tenant has had to leave a day early. Salmon fishery owners like to see their waters being fished steadily, to help maintain their catch averages (and thus the capital valuations of their assets), and this is where the standby fisher comes in. You may find yourself able to fish a beat costing £1000 per Rod per week for as little as £40 or £50 for a single day, and perhaps much less, provided you are on the spot and prepared to jump into the breach at very short notice. On many occasions I have arrived at Highland hotels a few days before the Twelfth of August and the start of grouse shooting, with time on my hands and with a salmon rod in the back of the car "just in case". A chat in the hotel bar, a visit to the local tackle shop or a telephone call to one or two local estate offices has never yet failed to secure me a day's fishing, usually at little more than the cost of a visitor's ticket for the neighbouring Town Water or the local Association stretch.

A fairly typical example of such a day occurred for me on Deeside on the eleventh of August, where I had arrived a day or two early, in preparation for a few days' grouse shooting to open the season. On arriving we had dropped a hint that we were in the market for a day or two's salmon fishing, and at breakfast next morning our host at the hotel announced that he had just made a telephone call and had managed to get my friend and me a day's fishing on a nearby and quite famous beat of the Dee. What better way of putting in the eve of the Twelfth? Ian went straight down to the bothy at the riverside and met the gillie, while I had first to drive south into Angus to meet the grousemoor keeper in preparation for the next day's shooting. It was a hot, cloudless day, and despite of a good height of water conditions were not looking especially propitious for fishing, so I enjoyed a leisurely run

The legendary Junction Pool on the River Tweed. Plenty of fine salmon fishing can be found at a fraction of the cost of renting famous beats like this one. (Painting by Shirley Carnt)

over Cairn o' Mount, lingered with the keeper, and was not back at the river until shortly after midday – to find that Ian already had a bright, fresh, 6-pound grilse on the bank. Inspired by this sight, I tackled up and began to work my way down the pool below the lunch hut, to meet with the firm take of an 11-pound fish after only a few casts – wonderful success in rather unpromising conditions and well worth our speculative inquiry at the hotel and the £30 we had each paid for the day's fishing. This is the sort of bargain day on a really good beat which can be had if you are in the right general area and your plans are flexible enough to allow you to grab your rod and go without delay.

"Have rod, will travel" is the motto of the opportunist salmon fisher, and he is a very lucky individual whose work and family commitments allow him the flexibility to drop everything and go fishing when an opportunity presents itself. And after you have accepted a few last-minute opportunities, the chances of sport grow by a kind of compound interest. Your name becomes known as someone who is able and willing to take a day's fishing at short notice, and if you are also a moderately capable and successful fisher, you may become a valued fall-back asset on the river, who is relied upon to fill in and fish a vacant rod and help maintain the fishing effort and the catch returns.

That is all very well if you happen to live close to salmon waters and can regulate your working schedule to fit in days fishing at short notice. But the same principle also applies to those who happen to live and work at some distance from the main salmon rivers of northern and western Britain. You may live several hundred miles away and be restricted to only a few precious weeks holiday each year, but if you let it be known among fishery owners, their agents, tackle shops, gillies and hotels that you are willing to take a last-minute offer, you may find that an out-of-the-blue phone call will get you onto excellent water at modest cost. I know of several such people, and groups of two or three fishing friends, who routinely book an August or September week on low-cost Association water somewhere on a Scottish river, while also letting it be known that they are ready to jump into their cars and take on a vacant private beat if it should suddenly become available. As a result of their flexibility, they often find themselves fishing unexpectedly good waters as substitutes for others who have had to cancel at short notice.

Fashion often dictates prices, in salmon fishing as in everything else, and as a general rule fishing on the big-name rivers will cost more than a similar spell on somewhere less celebrated. For example, Tweed, the Tay, the Spey, the Dee and the Helmsdale are all prime salmon rivers of great fame, where prices are generally high and demand exceeds supply. But other, less famous waters also yield a lot of fish and fun each season, although they do not hit the headlines so often. The rivers of the Solway Firth and Scotland's south-west, for example, have little of the fame of the great Highland and Grampian rivers, but they offer plenty of good fishing at moderate cost. In the vallies of the Esk, the Annan, the Nith, the Cree and the Bladnoch you may rent a cottage to sleep 4-6 people for £200 and have good flyfishing on your doorstep for around £15 per rod per day.

Wales, probably more famous for big seatrout than salmon, falls into much the same price range, while Ireland is still perhaps the best of all happy hunting grounds for the salmonfisher seeking sport on a shoestring. Lavishly hospitable farmhouse guesthouses offer all meals, including a packed lunch, for around £25-£30 a day, and a full seven days fishing may set you back no more than £75-£100 in all.

The west highlands of Scotland have a mass of short spate rivers that attract quantities of small salmon, grilse and seatrout from midsummer onwards, and the fishing is usually significantly cheaper by the day than a visit to a put-and-take rainbow trout fishery in southern England. You may need a spate and its aftermath to experience the best of the sport, but the seapools and lower reaches often repay a visit, even in low water conditions. And while you await that spate, fishing for wild brown trout in hill lochs provides an attractive alternative. The wilder and remoter places of the north and west of the British Isles can still offer lots of scope for the pursuit of truly wild game fish in sequestered and lonely places, a world removed from the crowded reservoirs and heavily stocked streams of the midlands and the south.

The costs of fishing are mainly influenced by two factors, in this order of importance – the timing of the runs of salmon, and the demand for fishing. It is only to be expected that a river or loch is most sought after when the fish are present and running in the greatest numbers, since that is when the chances of good catches are best. Likewise, there is much more demand for salmon fishing in the period from July to September, by those who are obliged to take their holidays then, than in the quieter months of February-June and again in October and November. Few British rivers now enjoy large early spring runs of fish, with the main spawning runs coming in the autumn, but many have large runs of grilse from April onwards. The delicately formed and maidenly one-sea-winter grilse may be smaller than a lordly multi-sea-winter salmon, but she is still every inch a salmon, and grilse enliven many rivers by their spring and early summer arrivals. This makes the late spring and early summer an exciting period for the salmon fisher, and less sought after – and therefore cheaper – since the decline in large early-run salmon.

Finally, do not overlook the potential of loch fishing for salmon. A

Spate rivers like this – Co. Antrim's River Bush – offer good sport at modest cost.

sizeable portion of this book is devoted to the special challenges and neglected potential of loch fishing; and if you book a week or two of fishing on a loch, there is always a fair chance that you may be able to get a day or two on the river as well, above or below the loch, if you happen to be on the spot and make it known that you are ready to take up any last-minute vacancy on the river that may occur during your stay.

This nice 7-pounder came from a peat-stained loch in early August. Drifting by boat over known lies is best, but this fish fell to a shore flyfisher casting into likely lies off rocky points and in sandy bays.

Chapter 4   Finding Salmon Fishing

The salmon fisheries of Britain and Ireland, large and small, famous and obscure, have been quite well documented since Victorian times, and a number of modern publications make a great deal of vital information readily available to us. *The Salmon Rivers of Scotland* by Derek Mills and Neil Graesser is a must for anyone fishing north of the Border, while Crawford Little's *The Salmon & Seatrout Fisheries of Scotland* is an important companion volume. Likewise, Peter O'Reilly's *Trout and Salmon Rivers of Ireland* and *Trout and Salmon Loughs of Ireland* are equally essential for anyone going fishing across the Irish Sea. (With due modesty, I might also suggest a glance at my own *A Game Fisher in Ireland*.) Full details of all these books are included in the Bibliography at the end of this book.

Nothing exactly comparable to these guides has been published in recent years on the salmon rivers of England and Wales, but most of the productive and accessible waters are regularly included in the monthly fishing reports published in the specialist game fishing magazines, including *Trout and Salmon* and *Salmon, Trout and Seatrout*.

Also published in these and similar periodicals are large numbers of useful small advertisements, which usually appear in the back pages, and offer salmon and other forms of game fishing throughout the British Isles, often linked to accommodation such as hotels, lodges, guest houses and bed-and-breakfast places. In a typical issue these magazine advertisements will offer you a wide choice of river and loch fisheries from Cornwall to Shetland, and from Kerry to Northumberland.

A couple of hours working through two or three recent issues of these magazines with paper and pencil to hand will enable you to build up a list of those advertisements which particularly take your fancy. The next stage is make a shortlist, and then write or telephone for more information. A letter is perhaps the best initial approach, as you can set out the questions you particularly want to ask, about the nature and extent of the waters, the likelihood of good sport at the times you are free to go there, the average catch rate in previous seasons, and many other queries that may come to mind. If the reply seems encouraging and you want to proceed further with your inquiries, telephone and try to speak to someone who can give you full up-to-date information about the fishery, its recent sport, and the likely

opportunities for the dates you have in mind. It is a good idea to have a written list of your questions, so you can make notes while on the phone. As always, when buying anything, remember the principle of *caveat emptor* – "let the buyer be cautious". Beware glib and silver-tongued salesmen who may promise you world-class fishing for a tenner a day, and make a careful appraisal of all the information you are given. Best of all, try to speak directly to someone who has fished there before, preferably quite recently, and can give you a candid account of what to expect.

In addition to sifting through the adverts in fishing magazines, be sure to pick the brains of all your fishing friends, of those whom you may meet in chance encounters while fishing, and of tackle dealers. The latter, by the nature of their work, are continually meeting streams of fishers and will usually have had an up to date briefing on the successes and disappointments experienced on a large selection of waters. Tackle sellers

Pick the brains of local experts. Charles Jardine (*left*) deep in conversation with Thomas Kelly on Ireland's River Drowes, a prolific grilse fishery.

often fulfil the function of piscatorial father-confessors to their customers, who are often dying to unburden their disappointments or reveal their triumphs to a receptive ear. In addition, most tackle shop owners are also keen fishermen. The gossip in a tackle shop is always worth hearing, and many lasting fishing friendships have been made across their counters and between visiting customers.

A visit to any new piece of water is always exciting, but it is bound to be more informative and productive if you have the company of a friend who has fished there before, or of the fishery owner, or of a local gillie or boatman who has intimate local knowledge. Their hard-won local knowledge accumulated over many years can put you right straight away, and time is very valuable when you have only managed to grab a few days of your precious free time to go fishing.

As a general rule, salmon fishing is likely to be expensive and may have been booked up for years ahead on the most celebrated rivers and the best known beats. They tend to have a reputation and a prestige which ensures that they will never lack high-paying clients. But bear in mind that vacancies do occasionally occur, often at very short notice. Personal or business problems of many kinds may cause a regular tenant to drop out at short notice, and there may be an unexpected vacancy, provided you are able to move quickly and take it up without delay. If you are able to take time off at very short notice it is well worth getting sporting agents, estate offices, tackle shops and hotels to take a note of your name and telephone number, emphasising to them that you are willing to accept last-minute offers. An out-of-the-blue phone call on a Saturday evening may mean you find yourself on a prime beat on Monday morning, and costs may be quite modest.

Fisheries owners and their agents are concerned above all to ensure that the water is being fished. Vacant days and idle beats mean reduced rod catches, lower average returns for the season, and a consequent loss of notional capital valuations and prestige. If a prime-time tenant fails to turn up and can be replaced at short notice, the replacement fisher may find that the costs are relatively very low. And if you can build up a reputation as a reliable stand-by, the offers of fishing may come along quite frequently. Of course, not everyone is either willing or able to drop everything and dash off fishing at a moment's notice, but if you can possibly do so the result may be some memorable sport, and all the sweeter because it was unexpected.

Some association and "public" waters, and some day ticket fisheries, can become a little crowded, especially when word gets around that fish are being caught, and also at popular holiday times and weekends when local people and visitors are free to go fishing. By 9am there may already be two or three Rods on the water, and many more by lunchtime and throughout the afternoon. At such times the early bird is likely to be the one who catches the fish, and it can pay handsomely to start fishing as early as the fishery regulations allow. Fresh fish often move into a river, or move up from one beat into another, during the night, and this is particularly true where the fishery is quite close to the mouth of the river and when there has been a high tide overnight.

Fresh fish will move inshore and enter the river on a rising tide, and these fresh salmon and grilse are renowned as very free takers of a fly once they have paused and settled in their first lies and resting places in the river. The first fisher down the pool usually has the very best chance of success, and that may mean rising very early to ensure you are on the water and ready to start fishing, sometimes as early as first light. This is particularly true of popular and heavily fished waters such as the River Drowes in the west of Ireland, where a majority of the abundant summer grilse fall to the flies of the early risers. So if you like to fish "gentlemen's hours", arriving at the water at 10 o'clock and leaving for a leisurely pre-dinner bath at 6 o'clock, stick to the more exclusive private beats, or be prepared to miss the richest pickings on association and public waters. Dedication and perseverance are essential for success with salmon, and this includes being prepared to accept that you must go fishing at some odd hours, heedless of normal sleeping and eating times.

Lochs offer excellent salmon fishing, often at low cost, and are often overlooked by river salmon fishers.

On waters where salmon occur, most of the fishing effort is concentrated on the main sections of the river. Many important tributaries of salmon rivers are only lightly fished by comparison, and some of the less accessible headwaters and also the lower tidal sections may be almost totally neglected. There is less cachet, and therefore lower costs, in fishing a small tributary than on the main river, and many fishers largely overlook the potential of lochs and tidal waters. Loch fishing, as we have noted, is often either underrated or is simply not to the taste of river flyfishers, and to go salmon fishing along the seaweedy shores of an estuary simply never occurs to some people. Yet many lochs are most productive, and every salmon that enters a river must first pass through the brackish waters of the estuary. (But remember the corrosive potential of saltwater, and take great care of your tackle accordingly.)

Once you have found and tried a piece of water that is to your taste, stick with it, at least for a season or two. Get to know its changing moods and characteristics through the year. There is no substitute for the intimate knowledge that comes from frequent fishing of particular stretch, and the rewards will be tangible in terms of fish on the bank, and of sheer fishing pleasure. There is always a temptation to try a new piece of fishing, on the principle that far-off fields so often seem greener, especially if your first choice has been blank. For a novice or even a fairly experienced fisher to keep chopping and changing rivers in search of better sport is usually a mistake, especially if others are managing to take fish from waters where you are having poor sport. It is far better to persevere and achieve a thorough working knowledge of one beat than to chase elusive success by flitting from place to place. Success will come eventually, and in the meantime you are steadily building up a basis of skill and understanding that will eventually enable you to approach any unfamiliar piece of water with a fair degree of confidence.

Chapter 5   Tackle –
general principles

The cost of tackle can be one of the intimidating elements facing the newcomer to salmon flyfishing. It can be a depressing experience to leaf through a tackle catalogue and see superb rods at £500 and more, magnificent reels costing hundreds, and even some brands of chest waders at over £200. But the best fishing tackle has always tended to be expensive, just like the finest golf clubs, and as funds become available in future years every keen salmon fisher will want to upgrade his tackle so that he has the best available – which incidentally tends also to be the most pleasurable to use. Functional efficiency usually goes hand in hand with good balance, fine finish and a generally pleasing feel.

But there is absolutely no need for the newcomer to aim so high. What is required by the novice salmon flyfisher, and many an older hand whose salmon fishing may be limited to only a few days each season, is a workmanlike range of basic tackle which he can use effectively. This need not be unduly expensive, although it is probably only realistic to point out that you should budget for a basic tackle outlay of about £300-£350 – which my golfing friends tell me is considerably less than a bag of moderately good clubs.

Rods
Salmon fly rods are made in three principal materials – split cane (sometimes also called built cane or bamboo); glass fibre; and carbon fibre, together with its cousins graphite and boron.

Split cane is traditional and handsome, but it is heavy, especially in the longer lengths, and few flyfishers today will be prepared to wield a cane rod of 13 feet or more throughout a long fishing day. For sentimental reasons I occasionally take out my grandfather's 13-foot Hardy steel-cored cane rod and its matching reel. Its action is sweet and pleasing, but I never fail to be astonished by the effort required to handle it for more than an hour or two at a time. Rod, reel and line together weigh almost five pounds, compared with my 15-foot Bruce & Walker Merlin and its 4½-inch reel and line at a total of 28 ounces. There is an undeniable tactile pleasure in the easy action of a well made split-cane rod, and this material still has its small band of devoted followers. If such a rod should come your way, perhaps as a gift or an heirloom, keep it carefully and enjoy taking it out and handling it from time to time, and even have a few casts with it. But do not choose cane as your only or regular salmon rod, for you will be immediately hampered by its weight and will lose much of the efficiency and pleasure of a successful fishing day through simple fatigue.

Glass fibre rods, both solid and tubular, came along in the 1960s in the vanguard of the post-war technological development of synthetics and their application to modern fishing tackle design, and the comparative lightness and low cost of this new material found many ready converts among those who had previously used cane rods. But fibreglass rods had barely become common in the 1960s before carbon fibre and similar materials appeared in rod construction and swiftly established a clear dominance in the world of rodmaking, a position they have held ever since. Carbon rods have an unrivalled combination of lightness and power, and now that the early design problems and high costs have been largely overcome they offer quite the best combination of practical qualities for the flyfisher. Glass fibre salmon rods are still made, and many are in regular and effective use. There is no reason why a newcomer to salmon fishing should not be able to fish with pleasure and success with a good tubular fibreglass rod; but carbon fibre and associated materials are not necessarily much more expensive today, and they confer such obvious advantages that they must be the first choice of anyone looking along the rod racks in a tackle shop.

A good salmon fly rod has three functions to perform. It must be capable of acting as a spring for casting a longish and fairly accurate line, not only in the familiar overhead style but also in various rolling and switching modes, of which the most important are the single and double Spey techniques. It must further provide the flyfisher with the reach to allow him to alter or mend the position of his outstretched line on the water, and then to

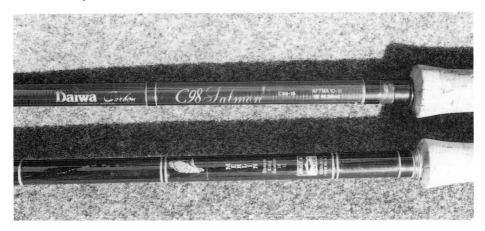

Two salmon fly rods. Note that each is marked above the handle with the maker's recommended weight of fly line.

In late spring, one flyfisher has chosen a single-handed rod for grilse, while the other prefers his longer, double-handed rod.

control the movement of the fly as it travels down and across the pool. Thirdly, it must supply the powerful yet sensitive leverage required to control and dominate a fish in play, and bring it safely to the net or the tailer.

By fairly general agreement, a two-handed rod of 15 feet is regarded as the ideal length for most salmon flyfishing on most rivers of the British Isles. (By contrast, American salmon flyfishers regard anything over 9 feet as long, very few use double-handed rods, and many use tiny rods of only 6 or 7 feet in length; but their style of fishing is very different and largely inapplicable to British and European conditions.) Rods of 16 and 17½ feet are not uncommon on our medium to large rivers and in heavy water conditions, and rods of up to 20 feet are available as standard production models from a few British makers. Shorter rods of 12 to 14 feet are commonly seen on smaller rivers, are popular with loch fishers, and can be a good choice when small summer salmon, grilse and seatrout are the quarry. And a single-handed rod of 9-10 feet can also be useful in certain conditions, as we shall see. However, for any adult man or woman of moderate fitness and physique, and for most well-grown teenagers, a 14-foot or 15-foot double-handed rod of carbon or graphite will provide the casting power and control needed for effective all-round salmon flyfishing, without being too heavy to be manageable.

If we take the popular 15-footer made of carbon fibre or graphite as our basis in looking for an all-round salmon rod, we must then be aware that considerable variations in weight, power, action, construction and cost are to be found within this category. Some specialist 15-footers such as the Bruce & Walker "Grilse" are designed for delicate fishing with very light lines in low water conditions, and are rated for lines #5 to #7. Others, especially the solidly constructed hexagonal rods such as the B&W Hexagraphs and the Merlin "Walker" series of thin-profile, thick-walled tubular carbon fibre, are rather heavier, much more stiff and powerful in the action, and designed for use with the heaviest lines of #11 and #12 weights, especially the fast sinking types used with large and heavy flies in deep, powerful water. The B&W Hugh Falkus 15' 4" "Sunk Line Special" is a good example of a rod of huge power designed for fishing a very heavy sinking line in the high-water conditions of spring and autumn. Both these types of rod are made with special conditions in mind, and neither is sufficiently versatile to be recommended for general use throughout a typical season. Something between these two extremes is best for general use.

Apart from the variations to be found in river conditions, individual flyfishers also differ in strength and physique, and often have marked personal preferences for rods with certain actions and handling

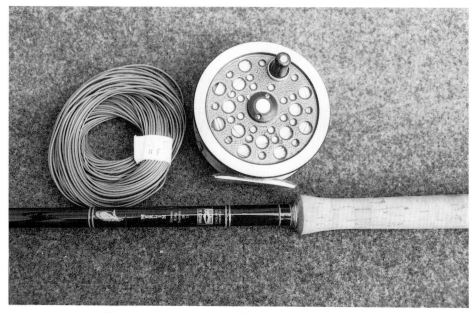

Look for the makers' weight markings to match the line to the rod.

characteristics. A sturdily-built six-footer is almost sure to have much more strength and stamina, and to be able to get more power out of a stiffly-built rod, than a lady angler several inches shorter and many stones lighter. And two flyfishers apparently well matched in size and strength may actually prefer to use rods which are quite different in action and style, one perhaps opting for a stiffish, fast action while the other finds that his style of fishing is best served by a rod with a softer, more languid action running right through the length of the rod to the butt.

Happily, carbon fibre lends itself to the construction of many different designs and actions of rods to cater for these preferences, and modern rod-making technology provides the intending purchaser with quite a wide choice. It is therefore worthwhile taking time and trouble to decide on the best rod for you before you part with your money. A wisely chosen rod which is suited to your physique and casting style will give pleasure in use, and a comfortable and happy fisherman is always more likely to be a successful fisherman. There is little pleasure in struggling with a rod which is a heavy, overly-powerful burden, or, conversely, in fighting to squeeze yet more power and a few feet more in distance casting out of an unduly soft-actioned rod.

Pre-eminently among British rodmakers, the firm of Bruce & Walker have designed a large range of salmon fly rods with these individual preferences firmly in mind. The matter is exemplified by the personal preferences of the two founding directors, Jim Bruce and Ken Walker, who respectively opt for rods with a gentle through-action and a powerful, stiff action. They have built upon their own preferences in designing a range of rods which cater for a wide variety of individual tastes, physiques and casting styles. Their hexagonally constructed Hexagraph rods have been hailed as market leaders since their appearance in the mid-1980s, and their more recent Merlin series has presented tubular rods in a powerful but slender form, with minimal wind resistance when casting. These rods are not cheap, but they represent probably the best design and construction currently available.

Ideally, a newcomer to salmon flyfishing will place himself in the hands of a competent and qualified casting instructor, for basic grounding in casting techniques with a long, double-handed rod. In addition to teaching casting, a capable instructor will be able to assess his pupil's needs, and may also be able to let the trainee try casting with a variety of rods of differing actions. In this way the pupil and his coach can jointly decide on the optimum type of rod for that individual's needs. Rods can also be borrowed from friends, are often available for test casting at game fairs and country shows, and can even be tried on the premises of a few tackle dealers lucky enough to have their premises close to a suitable piece of water. It is worth taking advantage of every chance to try and test others' rods, provided you always remember to take into account the differences in the weights of lines and reels used with them. Try to eliminate these variables, and bear in mind that a rod fitted with a narrow-drum, lightweight reel and a #10 floating line will feel and behave substantially differently when it is fitted with a large, wide-spool reel and a #12 sinking line with abundant backing line.

The "average salmon fisher" is an elusive creature and difficult to picture, and it is perhaps hazardous to prescribe the best tackle for such a chimera. But I shall put my head on the block and venture to suggest that a 14-foot or 15-foot tubular carbon rod of medium action and rated for a #19 to #11 line will probably suit most adult fishers under most conditions. Among low to medium priced rods of this type and readily available at the time of writing (1994) are the following:

> Daiwa CF98
> Daiwa Powermesh CWF15
> Shakespeare 450 Golden Fly
> Bob Church 15' Salar

All of these fall within the range £100-£150, are constructed in three sections, and perform as good, workmanlike tools with sinking and floating lines, and casting in both overhead and Spey styles.

Is second-hand tackle, including rods, worth considering? There will always be risks in buying a secondhand salmon rod, especially if it is made from carbon fibre and the rod's history is unknown to you. A hairline crack, perhaps the result of an earlier knock, may suddenly give way and leave you holding an irreparably shattered rod, with no maker's warranty to fall back on. But useful savings can nevertheless be made on expensive rods by buying from the second-hand selections offered by some leading tackle dealers, especially if they are prepared to guarantee the soundness of the rods they sell. One such is John Norris of Penrith, who advertises regularly in the game fishing magazines, and whose well-known shop in Penrith is almost a mandatory pull-in for salmon fishers heading north up the M6 en route for the Scottish rivers. A good range of selected used rods is always on display, and you can buy with some confidence.

Whatever your choice, new or secondhand, you should be able to equip yourself with a good three-piece 14-foot or 15-foot carbon fibre or graphite salmon fly rod for around £100-£150. And while you are in the shop, spend an extra £2 or so on a simple plastic carrying tube, to keep your rod sections intact when travelling. Something more expensive, like the superb adjustable Cromarty rod-case designed by David Parker, may come your way later, when funds permit.

A second salmon rod may seem like a luxury at this stage, especially for the beginner on a budget, but it is still worth considering; and the flyfisher who already has trouting experience may find that he already owns a suitable second salmon rod. By far the most useful second flyrod in a typical salmon-fishing armoury is a singlehanded rod of 10-10½ feet, rated for a #8 line and slightly stiff and moderately powerful in the action. This is suitable for fishing for grilse and small summer salmon in low water and on small rivers such as the innumerable spate streams of western Scotland and Ireland, where a day's fishing may yield a mixed basket of summer salmon, grilse and sea-trout. It is also an ideal tool with which to fish a sinking line using the technique known as "backing up" on large, deep, slow moving pools in larger rivers, which is a method we will look at in more detail later on. Such a rod is also excellent for fishing for salmon from a boat in a Hebridean loch or Irish lough, and it will also give good service for sea-trout fishing and sunk-line lure fishing for trout on stillwater fisheries – altogether a most versatile tool.

If I had the further luxury of a third choice in building up a comprehensive battery of salmon rods, I would undoubtedly choose a 12-12½-foot light two-handed rod, preferably in three sections for easy carriage, and rated for a #6 to #8 line. This type of rod can provide the delicacy of performance which is often so useful for summer salmon and grilse fishing in low water, where light lines and tiny flies are the order of the day. It can also be a most useful rod for loch fishing for salmon from a boat, another style of salmon fishing we will be looking at later.

Lines

The fly-line is arguably more important than any other component in the flyfisher's equipment. It is the critical link between the rod and the fish, which must be capable of fulfilling a number of essential functions. First, it must be heavy enough to "load" the springy rod and enable the fisher to propel his fly with sufficient energy and accuracy to cover the water well. Secondly, it must behave as desired in the water, riding high with minimum surface adhesion in the case of a floating line or sinking swiftly and evenly in the case of a fast sinker. In between are the slow sinkers, the neutral buoyancy or intermediate lines, and the sink-tip, which is a predominantly floating line tipped with a sinking section. Thirdly, the line should have a hard, smooth finish to allow it to flow easily through the rod rings with minimum friction or drag, so that line can be extended quickly and shot easily when casting. Fourthly, a good line will have a very slightly elastic quality to give a useful buffering effect against sudden shocks and hard takes, but it should also be sufficiently firm and stretch-resistant to keep the fisher closely in touch with his fly and a fish on the hook.

Level line

Double taper

Weight forward taper

Fly line profiles.

Lines for almost all forms of flyfishing are based on a typical length of 30 yards or metres, with additional backing or reserve line providing as much as 150 or 200 yards of further length as required. Specialised fly-lines as short as 12 yards or as long as 45 yards are used in certain situations. Lines are generally categorised according to three essential aspects of their design: their weight; their buoyancy (i.e. their sinking or floating characteristics); and their profile.

1. Weight: The weight of a particular line is always indicated by reference to a series of numbered ratings ranging from number one (the lowest and lightest) to number 12 (the heaviest in normal use). This system was devised by the Association of Fishing Tackle Manufacturers of America (AFTMA), and has been adopted as the international method of indicating line weight. The American "hash" symbol – # – is usually used to indicate the word "number" and thus a 10-weight line is designated AFTM #10. Line weight categories are reckoned by measuring the weight of 10 yards of the main fly line, excluding the level tip section, and it naturally follows that 10 yards of a very light trout fly-line will weigh a great deal less than a similar length of heavy salmon line intended for use on a much longer, stiffer and heavier rod. Modern rodmakers design and build their fly-rods with a certain optimum weight of line in mind, and this is usually indicated on each rod by a small printed or painted code number just above the top of the grip. Most salmon fly-rods will therefore be marked for the weight of line recommended by the maker, and thus a 15-foot rod for heavy work in high water may be marked AFTMA #11-12, while a 12-foot salmon rod for fine summer work in low water may be rated AFTMA #6-8. In each case the maker is indicating that a particular rod is designed to perform best when the designated weight of line is used on it.

It is essential for effective and comfortable casting that the line weight used should be correctly matched to the makers' indicated rating of the rod, modified by the length of line you expect to be casting with it. A line which is too light will not load the springiness of the rod sufficiently to cast properly, while a line that is too heavy will overload the rod. Remember, too, that differences in line weights also mean differences in the amount of line that has to be extended to load the spring of the rod. If a rod is rated for #9 to #11 lines, a significantly longer length of #9 line will have to be extended to achieve the same loading as a #11 line, with a #10 line requiring a length somewhere between the two extremes. If you are to fish a piece of water that calls for consistently long casting, you will wish to drop down to a slightly lighter line than for another beat that requires only short casts to be made. What counts is the weight of the total length of line you extend outside the tip ring. For this reason, the makers' line weight(s) as shown on the butt section is for guidance, and not for slavish obedience. Experience will soon reveal whether a particular rod and line combination is comfortable and suitable or not.

2. BUOYANCY: Fly lines are designed with different buoyancy character-istics to accommodate different fishing tactics and water conditions. Some are intended to float, riding high on the water's surface, and are therefore coded with the letter F. Others sink, some very fast and others more slowly, and are coded with the letter S. Some lines are designed with a sinking tip section of 10-15 feet on a floating line and are known as sink-tips, coded ST. Other lines are designed to float not on the surface but just beneath the surface film, and to have a virtually neutral buoyancy, and are coded as neutral or intermediate, with the letters N or I. Among sinking lines you may find considerable variety, with some designed to sink rather slowly, while others have a much higher density to promote rapid sinking for fishing deep in fast-flowing water. The line box or packaging will state whether a particular line is a fast or slow sinker, and may even give an indication of its sinking rate in inches per second.

3. PROFILE: Fly lines come in a variety of profiles, each indicated by code letters. L or LL indicates a line which is "level", i.e. of equal diameter and density throughout its length. Such lines have no apparent advantages and many obvious disadvantages for practical flyfishing, and, quite unlamented, they have now almost disappeared from the modern scene. DT stands for "double taper" and indicates that a line is tapered at each end, and symmetrical on either side of its mid-point, with the bulk of the line being of level or parallel profile but fining down to a smaller diameter and lighter weight for the final 12-15 feet at each end. DT lines are the most widely used and are available in sinking, floating and neutral styles, which means they are generally suitable for most forms of salmon flyfishing. A double-tapered line is essential for roll, switch and Spey casting.

WF stands for "weight forward", sometimes referred to as "forward taper", and indicates that the asymmetrical design consists of a long section of relatively fine, level line, bulking out to a heavier, thicker belly section at the forward end and then tapering back to a finer tip. This profile is highly favoured by still-water trout fishers, and enables long and accurate casts to

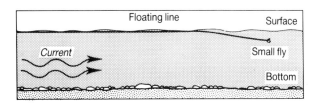

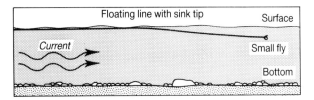

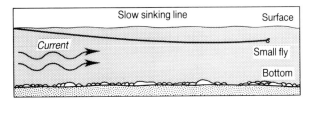

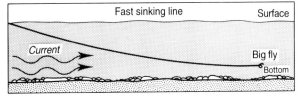

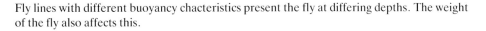

Fly lines with different buoyancy chacteristics present the fly at differing depths. The weight of the fly also affects this.

be made in the overhead mode, particularly when using single- or double-hauling techniques, but they are not generally favoured for salmon fishing, and their profile makes roll and Spey casting very difficult, sometimes to the point of impossibility.

These characteristics are common to all good ranges of well-made fly-lines, but the salmon fisher will usually have additional requirements. For effective Spey casting the line should be double-tapered, and for good Spey casting to maximum distances on biggish rivers the line should be 35 or 40 yards long with a long belly or level middle section. The dynamics of Spey casting make these important requirements.

Fly-lines for salmon are often advertised in the fishing press and offered in tackle shops at attractively low prices, frequently described as "mill ends" or seconds, and costing as little as £8-£10. Such lines can sometimes be good value, but too often they are simply a false economy, and they can prevent you from achieving your true potential in both distance and accuracy of casting, and in the optimum presentation of a fly. To use a rod with a cheap line is a little like trying to run a good car on low grade petrol: poor performance is almost quaranteed. With care a good fly line will last for two or three seasons, and sometimes much longer, and you should reckon on spending £35 or so. Spread over several seasons this represents a good investment. My own experience gives me a firm preference for the excellent lines made by Cortland and Scientific Anglers.

A floating line is the staple of most salmon flyfishers from late spring to autumn, and it is generally regarded as the most adaptable and enjoyable line to fish with; and both of these facts make a good floating line an indispensable part of basic flyfishing tackle for salmon. My own preference is for a Cortland 444F line or an AirCel Ultra 2. Floating lines tend to come in a variety of light colours, and pale tan, peach and light blue lines are especially easy to see, enabling you to follow the progress of the cast down the pool and control the working of the fly accordingly. Paradoxically, white floating lines are not always the easiest for the angler to see, and in bright weather they can give off a vivid flash on casting which I suspect may be potentially fish-frightening, and so I tend to avoid these for floating-line salmon fishing, keeping them for sunk-line fishing, or night fishing for seatrout.

Anyone with any serious experience of flyfishing for trout knows that the old divisions of the sport into dry fly fishing and wet fly fishing simply will not do. There are far too many permutations, combinations and variations for it to be subdivided quite so simply. There are floating flies which should be fished right on the surface, without a hint of drag, as imitations of emergent, egg-laying or dead adult insects. Others bob, skate or riffle along the surface in imitation of insect movements, or merely to provide an enticing attraction to lure a fish up to the surface. A so-called wet fly may be anything from a imitative pattern fished high in the surface film to a leaded lure allowed to sink to 30-40 feet, in search of deep-feeding trout, and bearing no particular resemblance to any natural food species. Nymphs can likewise be fished at depths from the top to the bottom of a river or stillwater. It all depends on the way they are presented, the size and weight of the individual flies, and the combination of leader and line with which they are fished. As for the latter, the modern fly fisher has a wide choice of lines within a spectrum which ranges from high floaters to ultra-high density deep sinkers.

The same principles apply to flyfishing for salmon. Too many accounts in books and magazines seem to oversimplify matters, dividing the sport into either fishing deep and slow with a large fly, a heavy leader and a fast sinking line, or fishing close to the surface with a small fly, a light leader and a floating line. In reality things are a great deal more subtle and variable than this. While there is no virtue in merely multiplying complexities for their own sake, it would be unfair not to give the newcomer to salmon flyfishing some idea of the range and versatility of the tackle and tactics now available.

During a typical season, and sometimes even in the course of a single day's fishing on just one beat, a salmon flyfisher may have good reasons to use a floating line, a medium-to-fast sinking line and a neutral density or intermediate line, with flies varying in size and weight from a tiny thing like a trout-fisher's wet fly, barely half an inch long and a few grains in weight, to a hefty Waddington or tubefly measuring 3 inches or more in length. All have their place, all will catch fish under certain conditions, and if the successful fisher is versatile in his methods, equipment and approach.

All this may sound as though the salmon flyfisher has to burden himself with a vast hamper of tackle, or be accompanied by a gillie laden down with kit like a Nepalese sherpa. Not so. A couple of pockets in a jacket or a fishing vest will suffice to hold two spare reel spools, each loaded with flylines with different buoyancy characteristics, while spools of monofil of different strengths for leaders and a few boxes of flies of a variety of weights, sizes and patterns need occupy no more than a few pockets. Travelling light is not incompatible with being comprehensively equipped.

By definition, a floating flyline floats. It has been designed so as to combine low mass with inherent buoyancy, usually brought about by the presence of a vast number of minute air bubbles within the tubular plastic sheath which enshrouds the line core. Modern lines usually also have a water repellent or hydrophobic surface finish, and the line is intended to float high up on top of the surface of the water, sitting on but not pushing down through the miniscus, that magical supportive film of surface tension. The ability of the miniscus to sustain material which is denser than water and will normally sink is something which most of us have seen demonstrated by scientific tricks, such as making an old-fashioned steel razor blade float supported on the surface tension of a glassful of water.

A flyline that floats nice and high should allow a clean and easy lift-off when you come to cast again, but for good casting some degree of adhesion and drag must be present. Every good cast begins with the backcast, and, in the case of an overhead cast, when the flyrod is raised and flicked backwards the line should immediately begin to load the spring of the rod by a combination of its weight and its drag (i.e. friction) on the water's surface. Only thus will the rod flex and build up the power to throw the line far out to the rear, ready for the second, forward power stroke which will load the rod a second time and in the other direction, to provide the energy to propel line, leader and fly out again. Therefore a really well designed floating line will combine characteristics of excellent buoyancy and also some "grip" on the water.

One of the greatest advantages of a fully floating line is the opportunities it gives the flyfisher to adjust the lie of his line on the water by repeated mending as the stream carries the line, leader and fly around and downstream. This enables the floating-line fisher to exercise a high degree of control over the speed and angle at which his fly is fishing, and such close fly control can put many a fish in the basket which would otherwise be missed. We shall be looking in more detail at mending the line in a later section.

Most manufacturers tend to offer their floating lines in rather light and pale colours, ranging from dark buff and pale green to peach, ice blue and snow white. One of the pleasures of fishing with a floating line is its visibility, which enables you to see most of your line and thus to follow the movement of your fly more accurately than with sub-surface lines. In virtually all conditions of light, from misty dawns to bright middays and back again to the gathering gloom of dusk, I have found that light tan, peach and greenish-yellow lines are consistently easy to see. But a very light coloured line, especially if it has a shiny plasticised coating, can give off a disconcertingly bright flash when casting is in progress, and the shiny white line is perhaps the worst offender in this respect. I am convinced that such line-flash is likely to be conspicuous to fish and may put them down, and I therefore tend to avoid them in favour of more sober hues. It is also worth mentioning that Polaroid glasses confer a great benefit in making your floating line highly visible, especially when there is a blindingly bright glitter off the water, and this makes it easier for the flyfisher to control the way his fly is fishing.

Next in the descending sequence from floaters to deep sinkers comes what is known as the "intermediate" or "neutral" line. This takes its name from its buoyancy characteristics, which are intended to be intermediate between those of floating and sinking lines, with the line sinking through the surface tension of the water and then hovering just below it, like a neutrally buoyant object. This is the theory, at any rate, but in my experience all such lines are in fact merely extremely slow sinkers. All will land on the surface and then cut quietly through the surface film, and their very slow rate of sinking gives the impression that they somehow hover just below the surface. This apparent hovering may indeed persist in the running water of a river, where the current creates a tension along the line, keeping it extended downstream of the rod-point, and holding it in the upper few inches of the water.

But use in a stillwater reveals that a so-called neutral line in fact simply goes on sinking at a very slow rate, of perhaps half an inch or so per second. This characteristic can be a definite bonus for the flyfisher, especially on occasions when the water is very clear, low and still, and when he wishes to make the least amount of surface disturbance, or when he wishes to get his line below the surface and out of reach of a gusty breeze which might pluck and twitch a fully floating line.

All the intermediate lines I have tried can be converted fairly readily into floaters by treating them with line floatant, which makes them quite adaptable. It is also possible to apply floatant to all but the final 10-15 feet of an intermediate line, thereby creating in effect a sink-tip line with a very slow sinking tip, and this may be a useful adaptation in some circumstances. But the natural tendency of every neutral line is to revert to being a very slow sinker after some further use, and they are best kept for this.

The sink tip fly line is, as the name suggests, something of a hybrid, consisting of a floating line with a tapered tip section of some 10-15 feet which has the characteristics of a slow to medium sinker, dropping in still water at a rate of about 2 inches per second. The extent of the sink tip is usually made clear by a change of line colour, and the sinking section is invariably darker in hue than the main flyline. The sink tip combines the visibility, easy lift-off and mendable qualities of a floating line with the comparative lack of disturbance which a sinking line causes, as it fishes with the leader and fly beneath the surface, and there can be benefits in keeping the more visible floating section of the line well away from the fish. There is also the great bonus of being able to mend the lie of most of the flyline, and thereby to exercise a useful degree of control as the cast is fished around.

Some makers now offer sink tip lines as a combination of intermediate main line with a sinking tip, which is a further variation on the many possibilities for variable density which modern line-making technology allows. An intermediate main line does not, of course, offer the same disturbance-free mending qualities as a full floater, but it is perfectly possible to treat the intermediate main line with floatant to facilitate mending.

There is a price to be paid for the combination of qualities found in a sink tip line, and this comes in the form of the sink-tip's rather unbalanced and disagreeable casting characteristics. Inevitably, the higher density forward sinking section is considerably heavier than would be the case with a straightforward double-tapered floater, and this destabilises the line when you are casting, causing the cast to go out and land on the water with rather a thumping splash. No-one would claim that a sink-tip is much of a pleasure to fish with, especially during a long day when you may have to cast scores and hundreds of times. However, a great many fishers have consistent success with this type of line, and will use it fairly regularly throughout the season.

Next come the true sinkers, all of which are designed in differing degrees to fish the fly below the water's surface. The genuinely slow-sinking lines have a very gradual rate of sinking, dropping in stillwater at the rate of barely an inch or so per second. Then we have the medium sinkers, with a sink rate in the region of 2-4 inches per second. Fast sinkers drop through the water at 5-6 inches per second, and any line with a faster sink rate can fairly claim to be an ultra-fast sinker.

Beyond this rate of sink we move into the specialised realms of ultra high density lines, which invariably incorporate a lead core, and these do not lend themselves to a line rating according to the usual AFTMA code used for more conventional lines. They are usually given a weight rating in grains, and the Cortland Line Company makes two such high density sinkers in this class, the Kerboom 450 grain and the 550 grain. These are designed for fishing a fly at great depth and perhaps also in a very powerful flow of water, such as may be called for on some of the massive salmon rivers of Norway, and they may have an occasional role to play on very big Scottish rivers such as Tweed and Tay in spring, when water levels are high and salmon are lying very deep. They are used as a relatively short shooting head, joined to a much lighter main running line of monofilament or braided nylon.

Reels

The salmon flyfisher's reel acts for ninety-nine per cent of the time as little more than a convenient store for the line and the backing, and many salmon fishers and writers on salmon fishing tend to regard it as a relatively unimportant piece of equipment, which can be bought without any great expenditure of thought or cash. Up to a point, this is true, but while a reel has a rather passive role while the angler is busy casting and fishing down a pool, it suddenly assumes an altogether more critical and active role when a fish takes. Once the hook has been set and a salmon is on, the generally approved technique is to wind all slack or hand-held line back onto the reel quickly and thereafter to play the fish off the reel. From this point onwards the reel is directly involved in following and mirroring the movements of a hooked fish right up to the moment of netting. Smooth, check-free running is essential if a strong fish making its first wild dash for freedom down the pool is not to meet with a sudden check as the spinning spool falters, and that can cause even a heavy leader to snap as if it were a thread of cotton. The bigger the fish the more likely it is that such a faltering check will be disastrous, and the more bitter the resulting disappointment. Smooth running is therefore a must, and the cheapest reels on the market are inevitably not constructed to the same mechanical standards as the more expensive models.

Reels large and small, showing differing drum widths.

Avoid false economy and buy a good reel by a reputable maker. The top-flight salmon reels made by Hardy, System Two and Orvis are superb but will cost well over £100. A more modest outlay of £35-£50 will still buy you an excellent reel from Bruce & Walker, Leeda, Young's or Orvis. The latter's modestly priced "Spey" model incorporates a synthetic disc brake similar to the metal disk used on their top-grade models and on the Leeda System Two reels, and seems especially good value. The more traditional ratchet-and-pawl braking system has stood the test of time, and is still to be found on many excellent reels. A well-designed salmon reel will have a carefully balanced drum, with either two winding handles at opposite sides of the outer face of the spool or with a single handle and a counterbalancing weight opposite to it. This promotes a balanced turning of the spool, just as a well-balanced car wheel spins smoothly, and avoids the juddering vibrations that can cause the spool to falter or check.

The resistance to line being pulled off the reel by the fish is known as the drag, and this is adjustable on many reels, allowing settings ranging from very light to quite heavy. This mechanical drag can be complemented or replaced by a manual resistance as the fisher applies hand pressure to the exposed rim of the reel spool, and most salmon fishers now favour such exposed rims in preference to the fully-caged reel designs which were typical a generation and more ago.

Since the 1960s the trend in the design of all fly reels, for every form of flyfishing, has been towards exposed spool rims. These have the advantage of being not only controlled by the mechanical drag or check mechanisms of the reel itself, but can also be readily governed by the additional resistance of the fisher's free hand. Cupped under the reel and pressing upwards against the exposed rim, the flyfisher's reel-hand can apply carefully judged degrees of pressure on a fish in play, and this pressure can be applied or released as quickly or as gradually as need be. Countless thousands of salmon have been successful and skilfully played off reels with wholly enclosed spools, but the subtle benefits of the exposed rim style are now firmly established for every type of flyfishing. It is now rather difficult to find any other style of modern salmon fly reel on offer from any notable maker.

When a powerful fish is played off the reel – i.e. without the fisher handlining a free length of flyline, but relying instead on the spool of the reel to recover or pay out line as required – a sudden fast rush can tear line and backing off in an astonishing rush, making the spool spin in a blur, while the drag or check screeches out the frenzied song that sends a tingling thrill through the flyfisher. Such powerful runs place great demands on a reel, and test the freedom and evenness with which it yields line. A momentary halt in its free running, or an unbalanced wobbling of the spinning spool, and the line may be momentarily checked in its outrun, placing intolerable tension on leader, fly or hook-hold, and a sudden

Insides of reels. The ratchet-and-pawl type drag (*left*) and the disc-type drag.

parting with the fish can too easily result. But the general standard of modern reel design is high, mechanical failures and inherent imbalances are few, and all but the very cheapest reels will serve you well. But the best reels, mainly at the top of the price range, tend to have the free running drags, the counterbalanced spools and the slick disc braking systems which inspire the greatest confidence. Nevertheless, the Leeda Magnum 140 and 200 models, and the Orvis Spey reels, incorporate these sophisticated modern features and still cost less than £50.

As we have seen, the flyfisher's basic armoury involves a selection of lines, and ideally each line will be on a separate reel of its own. This helps to spread the wear on moving parts over several reels, assists quick changes of line, and ensures that a fully serviceable replacement reel is on hand if a mishap or breakdown should put another reel out of action. Murphy's Law dictates that a reel breakdown will always occur when you are miles away from the nearest replacement, and it is therefore a good idea to acquire two or more reels as soon as funds permit, and keep a spare close at hand, as a backup. But reels are expensive, and it is therefore best for your budget to begin with a good reel body and two or three detachable spools. These cost about one-third as much as a reel and spool, take up slightly less room in a fishing bag or pocket, and can be quickly interchanged as required. When not in use on a reel, spare spools should be stored in small cloth or leather pouches (Orvis sell excellent "pokey bags" in suede leather) to keep the greased surfaces of cogs and drag systems free of grit, and to avoid unsightly scratches and damaging knocks. A rubber band slipped over the line will keep it all tidily in place and avoid unwinding and tangles.

A successful outfit for salmon flyfishing involves a harmonious marriage of rod, line and reel. If these three elements have been carefully chosen they will act in concert as a balanced unit, capable of being handled with little effort through a long day's fishing, and also able to cover the water well, to fish a fly effectively, to hook and play a salmon with a combination of power and sensitivity, and to bring it safely to the net. An unbalanced outfit will either mean an over-stressed rod if the line is too heavy, or else an under-stressed rod which a light line fails to load to full advantage. Frustration and unnecessary effort will afflict the flyfisher in either case, instead of the easy casting rhythm which accompanies a well balanced rod and line. The reel also plays an important role by balancing the rod, acting as a counterpoise weight to offset the pull of the extended line and the rod's leverage, while also allowing line to be readily released and easily recovered when a fish is in play.

On large and powerful rivers, where long casting, heavy water flow and big fish are to be encountered, the reel should be large enough to balance a long and powerful rod, at the upper end of the weight range, and to accommodate the considerable bulk of a 30- or 40-yard fly line, with a further 150-200 yards of 30-40 lb backing line. Such conditions are best fulfilled by a large diameter reel with a wide spool, capable of holding a great deal of backing line and of winding a heavy line in at a good speed. A large diameter obviously makes the latter task easier. On smaller rivers or in conditions which call for lighter tackle and perhaps for a shorter rod, a standard or narrow width spool, perhaps on a somewhat smaller reel, will be better, containing perhaps 30 yards of #10 line and 120 yards of backing, and with this bulking out to create a fairly large final diameter on the narrow spool, so that line can be wound in quickly if necessary.

For balance on a 10-foot single-handed rod, for use in small waters, a large trout reel or one designed for seatrout fishing may be best, capable of holding a 30-yard fly-line rated #8 or #9 and at least 100 yards of backing, and providing a good balance for the lighter, shorter rod.

A reel should be filled with line and backing so that the spool is well-filled but never overflowing when the line is fully wound in and the reel is detached from the rod. A reel which is only partly filled is not being used to maximum efficiency, for its reserves of backing may be too small, and the smaller working diameter of the partly loaded spool does not allow the line to be wound in as quickly as with a fully loaded spool. And an over-filled spool is a certain recipe for jamming the line and inviting disaster.

When winding a new length of line and backing onto your reel, the only sure way of achieving the optimum loading is to do it back-to-front. Begin with the tip of the fly line, loop it loosely around the central spindle or arbour of the reel spool, and wind it on fully. Then connect the backing line to the flyline, either using a good patent line connector or, even better, a needle knot or nail knot, finally covering the connection with a smear of superglue. This should be smoothed down to form a slick and streamlined joint which will offer minimum resistance and flow smoothly through the rod rings when a strong fish rips off line and backing. Then, firmly but gently, wind on as much backing as is required to fill the spool completely. Avoid joining various lengths of backing line together, as this entails making further connections and creating additional joins which may catch on a ring and snag the free flow of the line. It is therefore best to buy your backing line in joined spools, so that as one spool of line is used up another can be wound on without a join until you have the required amount.

When the spool is snugly filled, reverse the process. The most convenient way to do this is to tie the end of the backing to a fence or the branch of a tree, walk away and allow the backing line and fly line to be pulled completely off the spool, and let it all fall loose on the ground – preferably on a lawn or soft meadow grass rather than tarmac or bare earth, where potentially damaging grit particles can be picked up by either the flyline or the backing.

Take the now-empty reel and walk back to recover the tied-on end of the backing, and attach it firmly to the spool spindle or arbour. Wind on all the backing, applying steady but not heavy tension, and making sure the line is wound on level right across the width of the spool. Continue until the spool is full with backing and flyline, and your earlier reverse procedure will have ensured that the spool is now fully loaded, with the fly-line nicely filling the spool but not so much as to spill out over the rim.

Waders and Other Footwear
Wading is often essential for the salmon fisher, and one of the commonest caricature images of the salmon fisher is of a man immersed up to his armpits in a mighty torrent and flailing away with a vast rod. In fact, wading is an adjunct to successful fishing which must be carried out with thought and care. Many salmon pools and beats, and sometimes whole river systems, can be fished very thoroughly without the need to dip even a toe in the water, and for these a good pair of short boots will suffice. The Royal Hunter sporting boot with its studded soles is deservedly popular. Aigle make green calf-length boots with wire bonded into the soles, which provides a good non-slip grip, and the exquisitely comfortable leather-lined and zip-sided Chameau boots are incomparably comfortable, though very expensive. The ubiquitous green welly is cheap and serviceable, provided the sole is well-ridged and cleated for grip. Those with tungsten studs or interwoven steel fibres give really excellent footing in wet or greasy conditions.

The boat fisher for loch salmon will normally be able to stay dry-shod even in shoes, but may prefer to opt for short boots or lightweight thigh waders. The latter can be pulled up to act as waterproof leggings if it rains, but remember that fatal gap which usually remains between the top of the thighs and the hem of the waterproof coat. A wet, cold backside is demoralising and not conducive to enjoyable fishing, so take waterproof overtrousers as well. Beware tungsten-studded soles on boots and waders when fishing in a boat; they can leave deep scratches and gouged marks on the boards or the inside of the hull which will make you very unpopular with the boat's owner.

Felt-soled waders, once a rather specialised rarity, are now readily available at moderate prices from many waders makers, either as integral soles on one-piece body waders or on separate wading boots designed for use with bootless stocking-type body waders. Felt soles provide a wonderfully secure grip on almost every sort of river bottom, but can be very slippery on grass if you have a long walk to and from your car or fishing hut. Perhaps the best all-round formula is a combination of felt soles inset with a sprinkling of tungsten studs, and these are available off the shelf from several makers. Alternatively, you can buy sets of studded felt soles from Orvis and glue them to the soles of your existing waders or wading boots. These kits can also be used to repair waders with worn-out soles.

Thigh waders are of limited value to the river salmon fisher, except on the smallest spate streams, and it is better to choose a pair of good body waders. Many British trout fishers, emulating the American approach, are also increasingly turning to body waders for wild trout fishing, especially on rain-fed rivers. Modern chest- and body waders made from synthetics are pleasantly light and comfortable compared to the old type made from rubberised canvas, and an active fisher can walk considerable distances without feeling too hampered or tired. These full-length waders allow the deepest possible wading, up to the wearer's waist and a little beyond, and this is sometimes inevitable if you are to cover all the best water in certain pools on medium to large sized rivers. Even when you may not need to wade more than thigh-deep, these full-length waders, combined with suitable headgear and a short waterproof wading jacket, encase the salmon fisher against the worst of the rain and cold weather. They allow effective fishing to continue in foul conditions which might drive a less well-protected fisher back to the warmth of his car. The fisher who can defy the weather and keep his fly in the water longest – provided it is always fishing correctly – is the one who will fare best in terms of salmon on the bank.

When wading in the comparatively warm water of midsummer and early autumn rivers the usual type of synthetic body waders will be quite comfortable, and you may even appreciate a little coolness on a really warm summer's day. But in the chilly waters of spring and late autumn rivers you may quickly become chilly and uncomfortable, with numbness and stiffness making wading unpleasant and sometimes hazardous. If your budget will allow, the modern insulated neoprene and similar synthetic body waders are superbly warm even in the bone-chilling waters of a spring river fed by snowmelt from the hills. A cheaper alternative is to wear your usual non-insulated waders over two pairs of warm trousers and some insulated oversocks, and quilted sports trousers and tracksuit bottoms can be useful for this, perhaps coupled with thin thermal long-johns in really cold conditions. The multiple layers help trap warm air and reduce chilling.

Some perspiration and condensation inside body waders is inevitable, especially if the wearer has been exerting himself in warm weather, but clothing can be dried out and waders turned inside out to dry at the end of each day's fishing. Do not use crumpled newspaper, except as a quick initial measure to remove surplus moisture. When left inside waders it merely holds the damp in place and inhibits the free flow of air which is vital if the boots are to dry out thoroughly. At the end of a fishing day, waders which are damp with condensation or water which has come in over the tops should be turned inside out as far as possible, and hung up to dry overnight in a warm drying room. Most fishing hotels and lodges have good drying facilities, and a lot can also be achieved simply by draping boots and clothing close to a central heating boiler – but not on it! Avoid placing any equipment, especially waders, too close to extreme heat, which can do more harm than good by cracking or blistering synthetics and rubber and greatly shortening its useful life.

When deep wading you should always use a wading-staff, unless you have an intimate knowledge of the underwater contours and total confidence in your ability to keep your balance – and to save yourself if you do happen to slip and fall in. A good wading staff will be of a decent length – about five feet is ideal – and will be weighted at the bottom. This length enables you to feel ahead for obstacles and potholes on the river bed, and the weight keeps the staff upright in the water, in contact with the bottom, and well out of the way of any loops of fly-line. Mine is a simple hazel thumb-stick with a fork of red deer antler at the top and a short length of brass piping slipped over the tip and screwed in place, with a rubber ferrule covering the exposed tip and giving added grip. About 15 inches below the top of the shaft I have screwed in a simple eyelet, to which I connect a lanyard of light rope slung across my shoulders, with a snap-clip of the kind found on dog-leads. This allows me to let go of the staff when casting, when it simply lies in the water out of the way by my left side.

Although I am usually wary of two-in-one gadgets, which too often fail to do either job properly, I also like the wading staffs that incorporate a tailer in the head, just above the hand-grip. Once you have played a salmon, and are on the bank or in very shallow water, it is a simple matter to reverse the staff and use it as a long-handled tailer to secure your fish.

A longish wading staff has another benefit, which pays dividends if your muscles are inclined to protest after long hours of unaccustomed fishing, or if you are prone to back-ache, like me. It acts as a comfortable prop or third leg when held slightly ahead of you and to one side in your non-rod (usually left) hand when you are fishing out a cast, helping to maintain an erect posture and minimise strain on the muscles of the back.

To go deep wading in safety calls for care. Even so, it is almost inevitable that the day will come when you will slip and lose your footing, and it is then that your actions and equipment can mean the difference between a mere ducking and a tragedy. First, it is a popular myth that body waders fill with water and drag you down, for water-filled waders are only heavy when out of the water, and not in it. But if you lose your footing and slip into the water there are real risks of being swept away out of control in a fast flow, and if you should strike your head on a rock, unconsciousness may be the

Inflatable buoyancy vests and flotation harnesses can avert a tragedy if you should happen to take a tumble.

result. An unconscious body in the water will breathe by reflex and inhale water, and . . . The implications are horrifyingly clear.

Various neat and effective buoyancy aids are now available, including the Heron range of flotation waistcoats, and also the Shakespeare and Hardy inflatable fishing waistcoats, which can either be inflated by mouth before starting to fish, or instantly by ripping at a release cord which fills the Mae West-type lifejacket with CO_2, or, in the case of the Hardy model, automatically when the built-in sensor is immersed in water. The excellent "Sospender" and Musto wading braces are similarly inflatable orally or from a small CO_2 canister, and they are neat and unobtrusive in use, but inflate and provide a buoyant and bright collar around the wearer's head and neck when the tab is pulled.

Some useful smaller extras complete our equipment. Dark glasses are a great comfort, especially when there is a bright glitter off the water, and they can avert the splitting headaches which hours of exposure to light reflected off water can induce. Polarising lenses are best of all, enabling you to see your line and the movement of the fly when glittering reflections might otherwise allow you to see little or nothing. They can also confer great benefits even in quite dull and overcast conditions, and many salmon fishers wear them virtually all the time. Polaroids have become accepted as an almost essential part of every trout flyfisher's equipment, and their value in salmon fishing is equally significant.

Polaroid specs, fishing scissors, a whistle and other easily carried extras mean comfort, convenience and safety when fishing.

Best of all, perhaps, is the type of spectacle which combines Polaroid lenses with side safety pieces to protect the corners of the wearer's eyes. Any fly is a potential hazard when it is being cast, and a heavy salmon fly can travel at great speed and with potentially devastating effect. Although a good casting technique should keep you safe, an inept cast or a sharp gust of wind can deflect the fly, perhaps with serious results. Good fishing specs can avert serious injury.

Hats come in many styles, but there is a lot to be said for the traditional Scottish deerstalker, with its protecting peaks fore and aft, and its ear flaps which can be tied up when it is mild and tied down to cover the ears in cold conditions. But both the deerstalker and its close relative, the flapless "twa-snooted bonnet", can cause problems with their rear peaks if you try to pull a hood up over them, and a simple flat tweed cap is best with any type of hood, perhaps substituting a balaclava in really cold conditions. A splendid compromise is a flat cap made in the so-called Bugatti style, with no rear peak and with two ear flaps and a rear collar which can be pulled down and the flaps buttoned in place under the chin. In cold winds this encases your head, ears and neck, all of which can suffer serious heat loss, and if a shower begins you can simply pull up the hood of your waterproof jacket and continue fishing comfortably.

A small pair of scissors or one of the multi-tool fishing clippers for cutting leaders and trimming knots can be slung on a cord around the neck; and it can be a good idea also to string a whistle on the same lanyard too. The "Acme Thunderer" type of referees' whistle or something equally loud can come in handy when you need to attract the attention of a gillie or another fisherman to come and help you net a big fish – or simply to alert them to the fact that you have just fallen in and would appreciate a helping hand without delay! The noise of rushing water can sometimes make shouts for assistance inaudible. If, like me, you enjoy having your dogs nearby when you are fishing, perhaps basking in the sun or digging for rabbits or fieldmice along the grassy banks, string their whistle on your lanyard too, so you can keep them under control.

In the pockets of your fishing jacket – or, if the sun is blazing down, in the breast pocket of your shirt – you need only have a spool of monofilament for leaders, and a small box of replacement flies, to be completely kitted out. Other items of tackle can safely be left in your fishing bag on the bank, at least until you have covered that pool and prepare to move on to another. I leave such matters as smokeables, peppermints and spirit flasks to the individual's own discretion!

Nets, tailers and gaffs:

Extracting a beaten fish from the water is the culmination of a successful spell of fishing, and it is a critical point in the proceeding when all too many fish are lost at the very last minute, usually due to clumsiness or careless-ness. Many experienced salmon fishers never carry a net or any device for lifting out the fish, relying on their ability to bring the played-out fish to hand and tail it by grasping it firmly around the slim wrist of the tail. Where the beaten fish can be brought in to a gently shelving bank of sand or shingle this is fine, and the fisher need only keep tension on the line with one hand hold the rod aloft, while with the other hand he pushes the fish up clear of the water and then grasps it securely around the wrist of the tail. Where

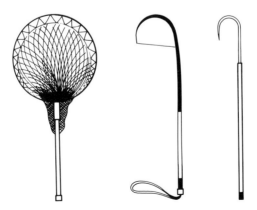

A net, a tailer and a gaff. Gaffs are fast disappearing, unlamented, from the fishing scene.

banks are high, tailing may be very much more difficult, and that is when a net or a tailer can be extremely useful. A tailer is simply a noose of springy wire that is set to form a large D-shaped loop, which is slipped over the fish's tail and then pulled sharply closed, the wire loop snapping tight around the wrist of the fish's tail and allowing the fisher or his companion or gillie to lift it clear of the water and well up onto the bank. Many tailers have extendable telescopic handles, while, as has been mentioned, others can be fixed to the top of a wading staff.

A suitable landing net for salmon will have a wide diameter, preferably not less than 30 inches as a minimum. What could be worse than losing a large fish because the net was too small? Thirty inches is also a minimum depth for the bag of the net, which should be capable of containing the entire body of all but the biggest fish, so that the salmon can be lifted safely from the water with no risk of its toppling out and back into the water, which may be the last you will see of it. When fishing from a boat, or if a gillie is with you on a river, the net can have a long fixed handle, but this is cumbersome and inappropriate when you are fishing alone. Telescopic handles must be viewed with caution, since many designs lack strength when extended, and some have a tendency to slide closed at the worst possible moment. The Gye-type net is widely popular, and is a clever but simple design which has a sliding one-piece handle that locks in position across the diameter of the net when it is not in use, and pulls out to form a robust handle when you need to net a fish. Most come supplied with a simple and ingenious sling or harness of leather or nylon webbing, that enables you to wear it slung over your back, even when deep wading, yet allows you to bring it into action with one hand when the time comes to use it.

The gaff – a fixed or telescopic handle ending with a steel hook with a gape of 4-6 inches – has all but vanished from the modern British fishing scene. Apart from its obvious unsuitability when there are either kelts in the river or gravid females close to spawning, both of which should be returned undamaged to the water, the gaff is an unnecessarily brutal instrument for extracting a fish from the water, and makes an ugly puncture in the flanks of an otherwise handsome creature. Its passing is quite unlamented, and all gaffs are best relegated to collections of old fishing tackle or as wall-hanging decorations in fishing pubs.

Finally, with your salmon safely on the bank or in the boat, use a weighted priest to despatch it quickly and humanely. Priests come in many shapes and sizes, and many anglers like to make their own, which can be either very simple or highly finished and rather handsome. A short length of broom handle with a small, heavy chunk of lead piping slipped over the end is perfectly serviceable and costs virtually nothing to make. Priests made from a length of stag's antler with a lead insert are attractive and not too expensive, and quite a few Scottish highland gillies make these in the winter for sale to their clients.

All this paraphernalia may suggest that the salmon fisher sets to business looking like the White Knight in *Alice in Wonderland*. There is indeed something a little knightly and gladiatorial (and often a bit comical) about the appearance of a bulkily clad figure clumping along encased in the rubber armour of body waders and carrying a long rod which bears a passing resemblance to a jousting lance, like some medieval tournament contender who has lost his horse. The vital thing, of course, is to be well equipped with the essentials, but not encumbered with too many non-essential extras. These can be left in your car, in a fishing hut, or on the bank. The salmon fisher taking to the water needs to be mobile, comfortable and carrying no more than the basic musts.

A Note on Clothing

"There is no such thing as bad weather, only inadequate clothing." The old adage of the outdoorsman applies to the salmon fisher, as to all field sportsmen. In the British Isles we enjoy the much-undervalued pleasures of weather that changes from day to day, and often from hour to hour. How different from – and how much preferable to – the tedious predictability of conditions in lands where they do not have daily weather but a predictable climate. Instead of the repetitive inevitability of dry seasons and wet seasons, hot seasons and cold seasons, Britain and Ireland offer continually changing weather. You may ply your flyrod on the Dee or the Spey in April and find yourself dripping with sweat, even in shirt-sleeves, while a September day may bring flurries of snow or pelting hail. Be prepared for continual and rapid changes of weather during the day, especially in hill country, and take clothing accordingly. Multiple thin layers of clothing that can be quickly added or removed provide the most versatile response to changes of temperature, while modern feather-light synthetic shell garments allow you to stay dry in torrential rain and sleet, without the clamminess of oilskins or oiled cotton. Remember the incontestable advice of countless gillies – "Ye'll only catch fish if yer flee's in the water" – and wear clothing that allows you to keep fishing when others retreat to the shelter of huts and cars. Salmon fishing time is precious, and good weatherproof clothing will keep you dry, warm and able to fish effectively in even the foulest of weather. Fish on the bank are the well deserved reward of those who persevere despite the worst the weather can throw at them, while fair weather flyfishers will seldom gain a reputation for consistent success with salmon throughout the season.

Most newcomers to flyfishing for salmon will probably already have most of the clothing and at least some of the tackle that is required, probably through previous experience with trout fishing and exposure to the elements. There is no reason why a budget of about £350 should not be adequate to equip you with the rod, line, reel and sundries discussed earlier, enabling you to approach what is probably the greatest gamefishing challenge with confidence.

Chapter 6   Rods and Reels

When assembling the flyrod, ensure that all the sections are lined up so that the line rings all fall in a dead straight line, and then push the joints snugly home, firmly but not with too much energy. Then carefully tape over each joint with plastic or fabric-based insulating tape. This should be wound on tightly so as to form a neat series of overlapping turns, and should extend for at least 3-4 inches to cover the joint and reach well down each of the sections. Fabric-based or non-stretch synthetic tape is quite the best, since any form of binding that is prone to stretching is likely to do so eventually, thereby allowing the jointed sections to move, which is precisely what binding is intended to prevent.

Taping is an essential precaution against joints working loose during the course of the day's fishing, or twisting and pulling the line-rings out of alignment. In a full day's fishing you will cast a great many times and the joints are subject to a great deal of repeated tension and torsion, especially if you are Spey casting. A joint that works loose is a nuisance at best, and may even cause part of the ferrule to snap, which will put a sudden end to your fishing until a repair is made. At the very least it will put an end to your fishing for a time, unless you happen to have a suitable substitute rod and line ready set up and near at hand.

For some reason, many flyfishers think that only salmon rods need to be taped. But salmon fishers do not have a monopoly of twisted or loosened rod joints, and every flyrod should be taped, as part of the regular procedure each time the rod is put up. Likewise, the taping should be regularly checked for any slackness during a day's fishing, and re-done if need be. It only takes a few moments to do it, and it can save a lot of frustration and even the expensive disaster of a broken rod.

When putting up a rod and threading the flyline through the rings, we have all at some time had the maddening experience of momentarily loosening our grip on the line, only to see it slip from our fingers and run backwards out of all the rings, to land in a heap on the ground, which means we have to start all over again. This can be avoided quite easily by adopting a simple line threading procedure. Begin with the fly line doubled over and thread it through each ring as a double thickness. Any slackening of your grip will cause the line to flex outwards and this will lock it in place in the last ring you threaded it through, thereby preventing it from slithering down out of all the rings – a simple way of avoiding a lot of fumbling and irritation.

A reel that works loose or drops off can spell disaster. Tape the reel fittings for added security.

Once a salmon flyrod is assembled, the joints securely taped, the reel fitted and the line threaded through the rings, you will want to keep it up, at least until you have to travel a long way, perhaps back home at the end of your week's fishing holiday, or when setting off to try another river or loch at a distance. This usually involves transporting the set-up rod and line to and from the water each day, and perhaps several times each day if you take breaks away from the waterside for lunch and tea, and cannot leave your rod securely in a locked hut.

Transporting set-up rods by car is simplicity itself, thanks to the various types of clips and clamps which are now readily available. But there are good and bad ways of using clamps, and a few words of caution are in order. First, always mount the clamps towards the offside (i.e. driver's side) of the car, or perhaps along the centre axis of the car in the case of magnetic clips, to keep the rods well clear of any obstructions you may encounter by the side of a road or track. There is a real risk of rod damage when rods are clamped on the car roof, especially if your route to and from the river takes you along narrow lanes with overhanging trees and encroaching bushes. Twigs and branches can easily snag on rod tips, rings and fly lines, and many a rod has been shattered as a result. If you have to negotiate lanes and tracks like this en route to the water's side, it may be best to mount the rods with their points forward, and clearly visible to the driver, so he can steer clear of snags and obstructions.

But beware of travelling long distances or at speed with rod points forward. With a 15-foot salmon rod, or even with a 12-footer, there will be a longish overhanging and unsupported section, however long the roofline of your car may be and however far apart you position the clamps. Driving at speed, especially if a side-wind is blowing, will cause the rod tips to bend sideways repeatedly and in an alarming tight arc, and they may finally give way and snap under the strain.

When longer distances and higher speeds are involved, it is far better from every point of view to mount your rods so that the handles are pointing forward, reels uppermost, of course, and just above the driver's sun visor, with the rod tips overhanging to the rear. In this position you can travel even quite long distances in safety at normal road speeds. Do remember, however, that upward opening hatch-back doors and estate car tailgates can spring up and foul the rods, possibly doing serious damage to them.

When the car is stationary, watch out if anyone should walk around the rear of the car. It is all too easy for you, one of your passengers, or a passer-by to overlook the presence of one or two slender rods sticking out backwards, and to walk slap into them. This is always a particular risk when you stop for petrol, when either the driver or the pumps attendant may collide with the rods by mistake. Fix a trailing length of bright tape or some other conspicuous marker to the rod tip, to make it easier to see and avoid. Salmon rods are delicate and expensive, and although your tackle insurance policy may enable you to replace a broken rod, a break will probably cost you at least a day's fishing, especially if the accident happens when you are many miles from the nearest tackle shop and there isn't a spare rod to be found.

Another potential disaster is when a reel slips from its moorings, either in transit in car clamps or while you are actually fishing, and however good your rod's reel-fittings may be this can sometimes happen. Not much imagination is needed to envisage the anguish that ensues if your reel suddenly drops off while you are in contention with a good fish. Taping is the answer here, too, and it is a quick and easy precaution to wind a few firm turns of tape around the upper and lower reel fittings to ensure that all stays snugly in place. Again, this should be checked regularly, and retightened if any signs of slackness should develop.

The rod and reel combination, when properly put together and taped for safety, should give no problems in normal use, even after many days of repeated hard work. The reel and line, however, also deserve consideration and precautionary handling.

Almost every encounter between a flyfisher and a salmon involves times when the fish has to be given its head and allowed to rush off. One of the most characteristic features of playing salmon on fly tackle is the urgent, powerful and repeated dashes that the fish will try to make. Effective playing of a salmon involves the use of the rod's spring and the reel's drag to wear down the fish's energetic resistance progressively. Only the heaviest tackle and the most firmly-hooked fish can withstand sudden uncushioned shocks and abrupt jarring. But this can happen if, by unhappy chance, the loops of flyline wound on the reel should become jammed on top of one another, causing the reel to lock solid. Suddenly the progressive drag of the reel spool's controlled rotation is replaced by a solid resistance, and the full weight of the running fish bears upon the fly, leader and line. Usually this spells disaster as the hook pulls out, or the leader snaps – and no-one who has experienced that dreadful limpness of tackle and of spirits is likely to forget it.

The flyline is likely to be stripped off and rewound onto the reel many times during a day's fishing, especially if one or two fish have been played and have taken off large amounts of line and backing. It is not easy to remember to rewind every turn of line with due care, and in the heat of a busy battle with a lively fish it may be impossible. But there is a constant risk of loosely wound turns of line becoming entwined, which has all the makings of a jammed reel and a lost fish. It is therefore a wise policy to strip the fly line off and rewind it snugly and evenly several times in the course of a fishing day, and always immediately after each time a fish has been played. The same procedure is also a sensible precaution each morning before you set off for the river or loch. The lawn of your hotel or a grassy field by the water are ideal places across which to strip off your line and leader, and a good deal of backing, too, if you have had a lively fish in play, before rewinding it all carefully onto the reel. These precautions greatly minimise the risks of what should be a free-running line and spool suddenly slamming to a standstill when you have an energetic fish on the end.

Chapter 7   Of Hooks and Eyes, Knots and Leaders

The business end of the flyfisher's equipment, and the direct contact with the salmon in play, is the hook. The successful conclusion of the fish's take depends upon nothing less than the hook's ability to catch on the salmon's mouth, to find and retain a deep and secure hold, and to maintain that firm connection until the net has been slipped under the beaten fish and it is lifted clear of the water. Only then is it removed, as the fish finds its ultimate repose in the bass or creel, or, in the case of an unseasonable fish or a salmon on a catch-and-release fishery, before it is slipped back gently into the water and steadied awhile until it regains equilibrium and orientation in the water.

The majority of salmon flies are tied on one of three basic types of hook – the single iron, the double hook, and the treble-hooked design. Within these three broad categories there are many variations, involving both the length of the hook shank and the position of the hook or hooks in relation to the body of the fly and the bulk of the dressing.

The accompanying diagram shows the most commonly encountered examples of hook design and style. None enjoys a really dominant position in the varied world of salmon flyfishing, simply because so much depends

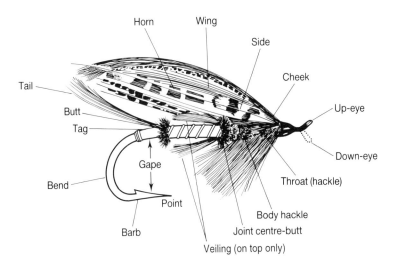

The anatomy of a traditional fully-dressed salmon fly.

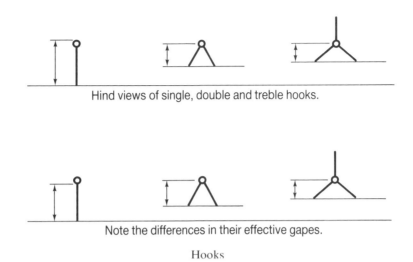

Hind views of single, double and treble hooks.

Note the differences in their effective gapes.

Hooks

upon the nature of the water to be fished, the angler's choice of fishing technique, the constraints of certain styles of fly pattern, and – not least – the failure of even the most experienced fishers to reach agreement on what design of hook offers the greatest advantages.

The diagram shows one of the most mechanically significant and widely discussed aspects of the hook debate, the variations that occur between singles, doubles and trebles as regards their gape and the extent of the grip they can afford. From the sketch it is easily seen that, size for size, the single hook offers the largest gape and potentially the biggest hook hold of all, and this was the predominant hook style used by our grandparents and by the designers and users of almost all the classic Victorian and Edwardian fly patterns, including many highly successful modern exponents of the single hook fly. But nowadays, a number of factors are frequently cited in opposition to it. The single hook may take a deep, firm hold, but for various reasons it is perhaps less likely to lodge in the fish's mouth in the first place. And once in place, its long and rigid shank may subsequently exert undue leverage on the precious hook-hold, perhaps causing the strain of fish and line to pull it out of place.

By comparison, the double hook appears at first glance to offer two chances of the hook finding a hold, while the treble hook arrangement offers three points and barbs, and, in the case of a tube- or Waddington-type design of fly, minimises the leverage factor as the body of the fly either slides up the line and out of the way (in the case of a tube-fly), or hinges and flexes barely a centimetre in front of the point where it is lodged in the salmon's mouth, and, in the case of the smaller hook sizes, even closer, as happens with Waddingtons and Brora-style designs.

In fact, all three styles have their places in the complete salmon flyfisher's armoury. The single hook can be ideal for very small, light patterns in low water, and also for large patterns, sometimes rather heavily dressed, in the higher, faster water of autumn, when a single hook is far less likely to snag in the constant debris of floating and sunken leaves that are borne down by the current at the season of leaf-fall.

The double hook, especially in the light, low-water style, is a firm favourite for summer salmon and grilse fishing, and it can be dressed in very light patterns without the hook unbalancing the fly.

The trebles of various types have great appeal for salmon flyfishers throughout the year. The out-pointed style devised by Partridge, and including the well-known Rob Wilson type of out-point Brora treble, have achieved a well deserved celebrity for their hooking and holding power, especially when used on Waddington-type spring and autumn patterns, and they can also be used with the tiny tube-fly patterns of high summer, when water conditions may be very low indeed. You have only to handle a few of these out-point trebles, or flies dressed using them, to appreciate their uncanny ability seemingly to reach out and grab you, or any other yielding surface in which their needle-sharp points can find a grip. They seem to have a magnetic quality, seizing and holding with a stiletto sharpness that can sometimes seem to have a life of its own.

Whatever the style or size, modern hook quality and design is generally of the highest standards, and a great deal of high-tech expertise in metallurgy and chemical tempering and sharpening has been applied to try and develop the perfect hook. Nevertheless, stones in the river, a snag on the bottom, or a flick against a bankside stone can easily weaken or break a hook, or turn and blunt the hook points. Consequently, every experienced flyfisher gets into the habit of regularly and carefully examining his hooks, especially when fishing rocky rivers, and always after the fly has hit a snag or become lodged on the bottom, however briefly. Often a quick touch with a tiny sharpening stone is all that is required to restore sharpness and hooking power to a blunted hook, and every flyfisher should carry one of these in his jacket or vest. Often they are included in the various multipurpose knives and other gadgets for the fisherman. And if a hook looks weak or one section of a multi-pointed hook actually breaks off, it is the work of just a few seconds to cut it off and replace it with a fresh fly. (Perhaps a little longer if your fingers are cold, or if you pause to admire the view!)

Whatever the hook style, the eye of the hook provides the point of attachment to the leader. The eye is usually formed by the wire of the hook shank being turned back on itself to form a more or less circular loop, and the attitude of the eye-loop may be in a direct line with the axis of the hook shank, or inclined upwards or downwards at an angle of about 30 degrees to

Tucked Half Blood Knot.

the shank. Most singles and doubles for salmon have up-eyes, while trebles designed for use with tube flies and Waddingtons have a straight eye, although the forward eye at the front end of a Waddington may be set at an angle.

A well designed hook that has a firm hold in the salmon's gristly mouth is all very well, but it is no use if the knot that joins it to the leader is inadequate. Whole books have been devoted to the subject of fishermen's knots, but only a small repertoire is needed by the flyfisher. For attaching the fly to the tip of the leader, or to a dropper if one of these is used on a two-fly cast, involves the choice of one of four knots – the turle, the tucked (or improved) turle, the half-blood and the tucked (or improved) half-blood. My own and many others' preferences are for one or other of the two tucked or "improved" knots. Opinions vary regarding the merits of the tucked turle and the tucked half-blood: it is claimed that the former creates a firmer linear link with the fly and helps it to swim on an even keel and in line with the leader, while others prefer the greater swinging freedom of the latter, claiming that it allows the fly greater mobility in the current. Either, when correctly tied, is firm and reliable to within something like 90% of the breaking strain of the leader line.

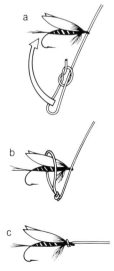

Turle Knot.

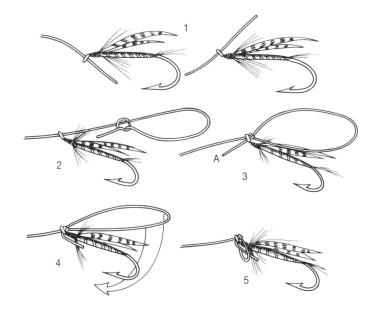

Tucked Turle Knot.

A further leader-to-fly knot is also worth mentioning, since it has occasional application when a specific style of fly presentation is required, and that is the hitch knot. This is designed to create an abrupt angle between the long axis of the fly and the direction of the leader's pull, and is variously known as the "riffling hitch", the "Newfoundland hitch" and the "Portland Creek hitch". Like all knots, it is much better described in a diagram than in words (*see diagram*).

The origin of the term "riffling hitch" lies in the way a fly attached like this creates a surface disturbance or wake – a riffle – when it is fished on or just below the water's surface. This type of knot, and the style of fly presentation that it gave rise to, is particularly associated with the Portland Creek area of Newfoundland, when British naval and army officers fished for the abundant Atlantic salmon in the prolific rivers there in the

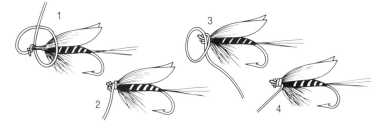

Riffling or Newfoundland Hitch.

nineteenth century. The gut-eyed flies of that era tended to weaken and, unless spotted in time, fail at the eye, and a quick expedient for repair was to tie the leader (gut, in those days) directly to the body of the fly, just behind the head, with the knot joining the leader at a right angle to the long axis of the hook, and with the fly in flowing water remaining quite asymmetrical *vis-a-vis* the main line and leader, at an angle of about 120 degrees. The result was a knot that was both robustly secure and also presented the fly in an unusually provocative riffling, wake-creating style that remains highly effective as a minor tactic in the salmon flyfisher's armoury, especially in the warm water conditions of summer. For flies to be hitched and fished to create a prominent wake on the surface in low water conditions, the best modern combination is probably to tie the hitch with the leader line first passing through a small hole pierced at 90 degrees through the synthetic tubing of the fly's body.

As a general principle, all anglers' knots, including the main flyline, any braided sections, and the monofilament of the leader tip and dropper, benefit from being well moistened before the knot's turns and coils are drawn tight to complete the knot. In part, this is a means of lubrication that facilitates the slick drawing together of the tightening lines; but more importantly it cools and eases the bonding of the knot, maintaining its strength and integrity when unlubricated friction might seriously weaken the connection. There are two very simple ways of doing this – by dipping the loosely entwined knot in the water, or by moistening the fully formed but still loose knot with saliva, by the simple expedient of sucking it in your mouth and moistening it thoroughly as a preliminary to pulling the knot tight. (Take great care that hooks do not become lodged in your tongue or

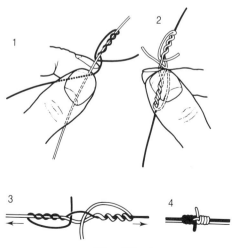

Blood Knot.

Tucked Blood Knot.

lips!) The result will be a knot that should draw tight smoothly and progressively without the damaging dry friction and consequent heating of the synthetic filaments that can so readily cause weakness in such knots.

Every knot slips to some extent just before it fails and the linkage finally parts. It follows that the tighter the knot is pulled when it is tied, the more effectively it can resist slippage when under extreme stress. The finer the line, the easier it is to draw the coils neatly and snugly together. Sea anglers who use large diameter, high breaking-strain monofil often have to resort to pliers to pull tight their knots, but freshwater flyfishing conditions mean that knots can usually be pulled tight with steady, firm manual tension. By the same token, the large diameter of the stronger monofilament lines makes it increasingly difficult to draw tight more than a few turns – perhaps only two or three – while a typical monofil leader of 10-15 lbs b.s. will pull snugly tight with five or six turns in, for example, a tucked half-blood knot.

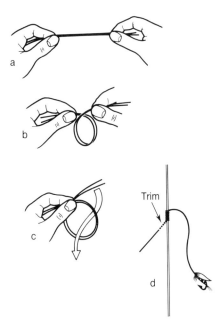

Surgeon's or Water Knot to join lines, or (d) to create a dropper.

In the 1980s there emerged a new style of monofil line, the double-strength or ultra-fine type. On the face of it, this development might have seemed the answer to every rod-and-line fisher's requirements, combining strength with delicate slenderness and near invisibility. What better way to minimise the fish-frightening potential of the leader than to make one that is much less bulky and visible, while sacrificing nothing in tensile strength? But fineness brought problems with conventional knots, and also serious inherent risks of severing by abrasion. This is a particularly serious disadvantage in salmon fishing, when the quarry is a powerful fish that often resorts to rubbing the fly and the leader against rocks and other underwater obstacles. Such unwelcome and potentially disastrous contacts between leader and rock are especially likely when fishing rocky, boulder-strewn spate streams such as are typical of western and northern Britain, and in Ireland, and the angler must take into account the abrasion resistance of his leader, as well as its lightness and the delicacy of presentation of the fly. Double-strength nylon is therefore of limited use to the salmon flyfisher, with the possible exception of fishing in very low water conditions with tiny flies, when only the finest of tactics are likely to bring success.

Trout and grayling flyfishers are, of course, familiar with monofil leaders which taper, providing a graduated and descending profile from the comparatively bulky tip of the main flyline, perhaps via a tapered braided leader, to either a single machine-made tapering length of monofil, or to a tippet that is made up of several shorter, knotted sections, in descending order of diameter and strength, to the final tippet point where the fly is attached. (A single machine-made length of tapered nylon will set you back about £2-£3 from a prestige tackle-maker, while a knotted leader can be made up by you, to your own requirements and design, for just a few pence.)

In general, the salmon flyfisher has less need of the carefully judged tapering and graduations of leaders that are so commonplace in trout fishing. For most of their fishing many experienced salmon fishers will simply choose one appropriate strength of normal monofil and use a single piece of this, of a rod's length or rather less, attached directly to the main fly line, or knotted to a fixed butt of heavy monofil between fly-line and leader. The better turn-over properties of a tapering leader confer little benefit when the fly is of a medium or heavy weight, in which case the forward momentum of the fly will draw the leader forwards and turn it over as line, leader and fly flow out on the forward stroke of the cast. For this reason, all the individual salmon flyfisher usually needs to carry for leader replacements or repairs is one handy spool of monofil of the requisite strength.

With the very small – size 10-16 – flies that are sometimes called for, everything becomes much more delicate and precise, and a neater turnover and more accurate presentation will be achieved with a tapered leader. In this case there is a choice of either a readymade, one-piece tapered leader, or else a knotted leader you can make up yourself from monofil of descending diameters and breaking strains.

The butt end of the leader can be attached either to the main fly line, or to a heavy butt of monofil, or a braided butt, by one of a selection of knots and loops.

Chapter 8   Water Conditions

Water conditions, and the salmon flyfisher's correct interpretation of them, are critical for success. After all, water is the fish's essential milieu, just as we are creatures that live and breathe in the earth's gaseous atmosphere. The quality of the water, its salinity, its purity, the speed of its flow, its temperature and the degree of oxygen saturation, and the extent to which its flow is increasing or decreasing, are all important factors that have a bearing on the movements and behaviour of salmon. It is therefore important to have some idea of how and why this is so, if time spent fishing is to be productive.

As we have seen in the section dealing with the natural history of the salmon, it is a creature that is continually adjusting itself to the changing circumstances of its watery environments. Perhaps the most critical of these, from the fisherman's point of view, is the general suppression of the salmon's feeding impulse when it runs in from the open sea, passes through an estuarine zone of brackish water, and re-enters the freshwater of the river system that it left as a smolt. Once back from the sea, the fish moves and acts in ways that are responsive to the conditions of its new environment of fresh, flowing water.

A good, steady flow will draw salmon further up the river system, ever onwards towards their eventual spawning areas, and a moderate water temperature – say 45°F-55°F – combined with a steadily maintained water speed will give the fish the energy and vitality to press onwards and circumvent obstacles such as weirs, low falls and shallows that might otherwise impede progress. Very cold river water makes the fish torpid and sluggish, while the high water temperatures of summer make the fish stale and unresponsive as they wait in the fast water and the comparative cool of the deeper pools until rainfall raises the river level and boosts the flow of well oxygenated water to enable them to move on.

High flood water may be fresh and rich in oxygen, but its surging power is wearying for the fish to swim against, and its swollen waters are probably also full of debris, silt, suspended peat particles and other detritus that "sicken the fish", as gillies often remark. In such conditions, salmon will tend to lie well out of the main current, close to the sides of the river and in the slacker flows beneath undercut banks, waiting for the flood to subside and the water to calm and clear again. Flood conditions mean poor fishing, but the period of the main spate is preceded and followed by spells when the rod fisherman's prospects can be very good indeed.

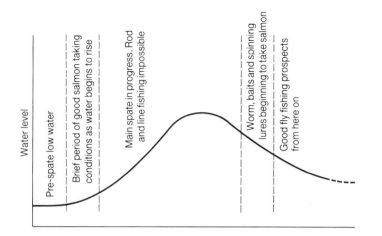

In a spate, salmon often display a brief taking time just as the river level begins to rise, after which the water is unfishable with a fly until the spate is well past its peak.

When a river begins to rise at the onset of a spate, there is a brief but valuable period when the fish detect the first hints of the coming flood and seem to be enlivened by it. This fleeting period often transforms unresponsive fish previously settled in their lies into active and eager movers, and a fly may be readily taken by a fish that would have ignored it just a few minutes earlier. On a beat where there is a good stock of fish resting in the pools, this pre-spate reaction can bring fast and furious sport as the first hints of rising water and a faster flow stimulate a brief period of ready taking. Then all goes dead as the water rises fast and the river colours-up quickly with its load of suspended sand, peat and silt, and sweeps down all kinds of flotsam from a long way upstream. That is the time to reel in and head for hotel or home until the water level begins to subside.

In the small salmon river systems of western and northern Scotland, of the West Country, and of much of Ireland, you may be able to predict the onset of a spate quite easily. Heavy rainclouds moving overhead as you fish may be evidence enough, and the steady beating of rain on your bedroom window during the night may predict that there will be no hurry to rise early and get to the river quickly. A leisurely breakfast and a morning's shopping or sightseeing may be much more enjoyable than contemplating the sight of an unfishable river in full spate. Spates on small western rivers can run off quickly, and waters that are unfishable in the morning may have dropped and cleared into excellent condition by late afternoon, providing good fishing until the light finally fades.

On large river systems it is not quite so easy to tell what may happen, since you may be enjoying shirt-sleeve conditions on one of the middle or lower beats of the Dee, the Spey, the Findhorn or the Cork Blackwater, wholly unaware that a prolonged storm has sent hundreds of tons of rainwater into the hilly headwaters many miles away upstream. The generalised weather forecasts on radio and television are seldom accurate in their predictions for the remoter corners of Britain and Ireland, and in upland areas the capricious weather can vary dramatically from one glen to the other side of the hills. On your dry and warm downstream beat you will do well to keep an eye on the gauge or that twig you carefully planted at the water's edge. There may even be occasions when all the warning you will get is when you hear the rumbling surge of a spate coming down behind you, or, worse, glance round to see a wall of storm-water rushing down towards you – in either of which cases get out of the water and well up the bank just as fast as you possibly can.

A sudden, massive spate like this can render a beat unfishable in a few moments, allowing no gradual rise in water level and rate of flow that can bring salmon on the take for a brief pre-spate "happy hour", and when this happens there is no alternative but to reel in and forget about fishing until the flood subsides. The same goes for rivers which are subject to sudden fluctuations of flow caused by hydroelectricity generating plants, although many hydro system operators are thoughtful enough to announce well in advance the times at which they intend to begin generating, and to supply a worthwhile compensation flow to keep the river fishable when the turbines are not working. But whenever you see that the river is rising slowly and the flow strengthening gradually, do not miss those fifteeen or twenty precious minutes when the fish may suddenly become very obliging. Some of the

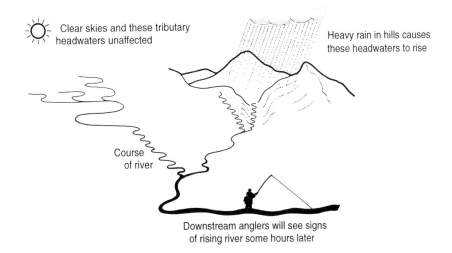

Localised rainfall later affects water heights far downstream. Note how the tributary remains unaffected.

most notable successes I have experienced during these short windows of opportunity have come as a result of quickly changing to a fly a size or two larger than the one I was using earlier, in steady water conditions.

All salmon fishing literature and lore proclaims that a river that is fining down after a flood offers the very best prospects for the fisherman. The opportunities come in stages, with the first drop in flow and height enticing the worm and prawn fishers into action, while the water may still be very turbid and powerful. The next stage encourages those who favour the spun lure – toby or Devon or "flying-C" – and can also be productive for the flyfisher who uses a very fast sinking line and a large Waddington or tube-type fly. To cope with a combination of a heavy, powerful flow, a fast-sinking line and a large fly calls for energy and determination, but may be richly rewarded. Other flyfishers may prefer to wait a bit longer, until the water has cleared to the colour of weak tea and the flow has become gentler. By then, the falling flood should have refreshed the whole length of the river with a flush of cool, well oxygenated water, a stimulus to the resident fish and an invitation for fresh salmon to move in from the estuary and beyond.

Each river has its own character, and some run off very much faster than others. One river may level out at a good fishing height for a week or more, as the aftermath of a spate soaks steadily down from the headwaters and maintains a more or less uniform depth and flow, while another may rise and fall again in a matter of a few hours. Geography and geology often explain this, and a very fast rise and subsequent run-off is often created or exacerbated when a river catchment has been extensively drained and ploughed for commercial afforestation. There are now vast areas of upland Britain and Ireland where heavy rain and flash floods on high ground are channelled immediately into the rivers by forest drainage networks, precipitating dramatic rises and equally swift falls in water levels on rivers where earlier generations of anglers had experienced much more gradual rises and falls in water height, with more extended periods of prime settled fishing conditions. There is not much to be done about these unfortunate changes, except to try and ensure that your fly is in the water during the critical period as the run-off drains away – and to campaign with the rest of the game fishing fraternity for a more sympathetic approach to forestry and upland drainage in the future. Conditions that spell spates or droughts in rivers have much less effect on salmon and salmon fishing in lochs, as is discussed in the section on fishing in still-waters. The often-neglected sporting potential of lochs deserves more recognition as a source of alternative salmon fishing when rivers are in poor order, in addition to their special appeal as excellent fisheries in their own right.

Chapter 9   The Temperature Factor

Salmon, like all fish and most other creatures which live in the sea or in freshwater, are cold-blooded. By this we mean that the temperature, of the air and especially of the water, plays a critical role in their life and behaviour which it is difficult to exaggerate. The salmon fisher who neglects to take into account the effects of temperature on the metabolic rate and thus the behaviour of his quarry will probably only catch salmon by accident.

Temperature affects almost every aspect of the salmon's life, from birth to death. The fertilised eggs buried in the gravelly redd by the spawning adults are critically influenced by water temperature, developing and hatching at a rate which is directly related to the warmth of the river water. In the warmish waters of Spanish and Portuguese rivers, which are at the southern limits of the salmon's European range, with average water temperatures of 10°C-11°C, incubation may take only about 40 days. In the chill 2°C rivers fed by snow-melt in Norway and Russia it may take between three and four times as long.

Alevins hatched into warm and nutrient-rich rivers grow much faster than their counterparts in cold and nutritionally impoverished waters, and they go on to progress more quickly through the successive fry and parr stages. The arrival of the critical stage of smoltation and migration to sea is also affected by the temperature of the river water. From the relatively warm rivers of southern England, France and Iberia the majority of smolts – over 90 per cent – migrate as yearlings, while smolts from colder, less food-rich rivers in northern Norway and north-east Canada will be between six and eight years old when they eventually drop downstream and out to sea. Research has indicated that a temperature of 7°C constitutes a critical threshold, and that smolt age is inversely related to the number of days in the year when the water temperature reaches or exceeds that point. Putting this another way, the smolt stage therefore comes earlier in rivers which have a greater number of days in the year on which the temperature reaches or exceeds 7°C.

During their lives at sea, salmon movements and behaviour are also related to the temperature of the water, and this varies in different parts of the Atlantic according to the presence of warm and cold currents, plus the inevitable warming and cooling of the surface layers of the ocean as the seasons of the year come and go. During the marine phase of their lives salmon are known as pelagic fish, living and feeding generally in the upper layers of the water – where, alas, far too many fall foul of drift nets. But salmon have also been taken in commercial nets at depths of over 250 feet, and have been monitored by scientists at still greater depths, and they seem to move deeper to feed when the water temperature is low, for example in areas where cold currents prevail, and where their principal food species are also living deeper in the water than they would if the temperature was higher. In cold water conditions salmon and their prey live deeper and also move more slowly than in warmer water. Predator and prey alike are under the influence of water temperatures.

Once they have returned as adults to spawn in the rivers of their youth, salmon do not cease to be similarly affected by temperature. Cold water in early spring, when the river may be fed by melt-water from the disappearing snows of winter, makes salmon move with slow and sluggish deliberation, and such fish are reluctant and are indeed metabolically incapable of pressing on up the river, especially if their passage involves surmounting falls and steep stretches of fast white water. Instead they will lie deep and almost moribund until a rise in water temperature speeds up their metabolisms and enables them to muster the energy and speed necessary to push onwards and upwards. For this reason many river systems hold almost all their early-run fish, and therefore show most of their early sport, in the lower pools and beats, where quite large numbers of early salmon annually wait below a high falls or a steep stretch of white water until the temperature of the water rises, to stimulate their energies and enable them to surmount what have hitherto been impossible barriers. Many rivers have these falls or rapids, which are known as "temperature barriers" in the early days of the season when the water is still cold, but which the fish can negotiate with ease once the water is warmer. Good examples of these temperature pools are to be found below the Kildonan falls on the Helmsdale in Sutherland, and the Gledfield falls on the Carron in Easter Ross.

Although salmon tend to become more lively and energetic as the water temperature rises in spring and early summer, there may come a point where river water, especially in a hot summer period with little or no rainfall, becomes unattractively warm, stale and deoxygenated, and such conditions can then induce renewed torpor and lethargy in salmon, making them all but uncatchable until a freshet of new, well-oxygenated water comes down the river, gingering them up and making them once again alert and receptive to a well presented fly.

Temperature affects not only the behaviour of salmon but also the activity of other forms of life in freshwaters. Other fish and invertebrates will also become more active as the water temperature rises, the whole tempo of the life of the river quickens, and this in turn affects how the salmon fisher should ply his fly.

The intention behind the presentation of a fly to a salmon is the angler's hope that it will somehow trigger off the fish's deep-seated impulse to feed on what it imagines to be a food species. It is generally accepted that salmon tend not to feed in freshwater, and that they undergo important metabolic and behavioural changes on returning from their saltwater feeding grounds to the freshwaters where they will eventually spawn. Suppression of the fish's appetite and of the impulse to feed is one of these changes. But suppression is not the same as elimination, and the fish probably does not entirely lose those impulses to feed which have been so effective in causing it to grow from a little smolt into a big, muscular fish after as little as one year at sea. As a post-spawner – a kelt – abstention quickly reverts to voracious appetite as the salmon switches back into feeding mode again. The challenge, therefore, is to present a fly to the fish in a manner which will trigger that suppressed but latent feeding urge, and cause the fish to take the fly like a food item. And if it should be prompted to grab it by another motive such as aggression or curiosity, the effect is the same – the salmon takes the fly into its mouth.

Later in the season, when spawning is imminent, the cock fishes' lower jaws develop their hooked kypes and become armed with big spawning teeth, and the comparative quiescence of spring and summer is largely replaced by more overt aggression and the frantic desire to drive off or destroy anything that is perceived as a threat or an enemy. It is this

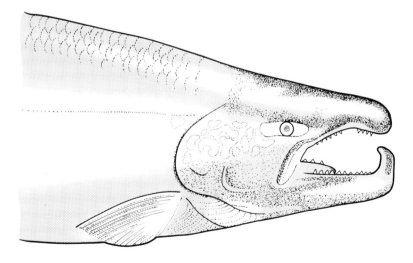

The pronounced hooked jaw or kype of a cock salmon in spawning condition.

behaviour, in defence of its mate or its chosen spawning territory, that will cause a late-season cock salmon to attack a fly or a lure with energy and little apparent discrimination.

Effective fly presentation involves showing the fish an object which arouses its aggression, or its curiosity, or which invokes its half-buried memories of desirable food species like those it fed upon at sea. This in turn depends upon the pattern and dressing of the fly, its colour, its size, and the way in which it moves in the water. To be convincing and attractive, the fly must look and act in a way which resembles and recalls some genuine salmon prey species, and this varies with the water temperature. In chill snow-melt water all the animate life of the river moves slowly, while the warmer climate of May and June is reflected in the brisker, free-moving energy of the creatures that live in the water, including both the salmon and the smaller fish.

If you cast a smallish fly – say, a one-inch tube fly – into a March river whose temperature is in the mid-30s you cannot expect it to behave in a way that is convincing to a salmon unless you make the fly fish very much more slowly than the same fly cast across the same pool in July or August, when the water temperature may be in the 60s. In cold water a small fish, such as the fly may represent, can only muster a fraction of the energy and swimming speed that it can demonstrate in warmer water, and in the slow-motion world of a chill river a salmon will find a fast-moving fly unnatural and unconvincing. Fished briskly on a warm summer day, that same fly might bring a salmon lunging many yards across a pool to take it with zest: in cold conditions it simply will not do. This fact must be mirrored in the way the flyfisher plies his fly.

In very cold water a large fly is not always necessary, but if a small pattern is used it has to be fished in a style and at a speed that are consistent with the natural behaviour of a little fish in water of that temperature. If the pace of the river's flow is three miles per hour, a fly that is simply hanging or dangling in the water appears static in relation to the fixed geography of the river, and to the salmon that is settled and sedentary in its lie, but in relation to the water it is maintaining an upstream speed of 3 mph so as to remain static. Any less and it would be carried downstream by the current. If the fly moves across the pool its relative swimming speed is even greater, since it is not only overcoming the current's flow but also making progress across the flow, perhaps equivalent to swimming at 4 mph. And as the angler slowly handlines the fly back upstream towards him before recasting, the fly gives the appearance of a small fish moving at perhaps 5 mph or slightly more. From the salmon's point of view, that is only convincing behaviour if a small fish could achieve and maintain the same speed under those conditions. A larger fish is capable of moving faster in cold water, and the flyfisher

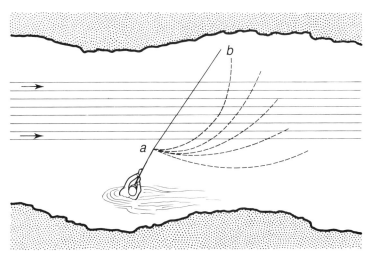

If the fly is cast from *a* to *b*, a pronounced belly will be formed. In fast water the fly
will move too quickly, but in slow flows the belly gives useful pace to the fly.

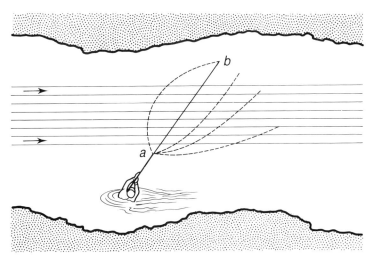

Following the cast *a* to *b* the angler should make an upstream 'mend' to make the
fly move more slowly for the remainder of its arc.

Speed of flies being fished.

continually has to match the size of the fly he uses to the speed at which he
fishes it at specific water temperatures.

For this reason, larger fly types tend to be more widely used in the cold
waters of early spring and late autumn, and these include not only large
Waddingtons and tube flies that may have an eye-to-hook length of three
inches and an overall dressed length of more than four inches, but also

After grilse in low water. When the water runs low and warm, salmon tend to lie in the better oxygenated riffles, often at the heads of pools.

patterns such as the Collie Dog, a favourite cold-water fly, that trails a long wing of 6-9 inches of hair. In the water this has an attractively sinuous movement and also gives the impression of a comparatively large fish, which is capable of moving at a much greater speed in cold water than a little fish approximating in size to our one-inch tube fly, for example.

Water condition in general, and temperature in particular, tends to change as the season progresses. The usual pattern is for water temperatures to rise gradually, peaking in July and early August, and dropping off gradually with the onset of autumn, the first frosts and the approaching end of the rod fishing season. Within this general pattern there will often be localised peaks and troughs, in response to the particular spells of weather, especially rainfall, affecting that river catchment.

When a river has received good runs of fish from early spring onwards, the salmon population will be substantial by the end of May and early June. On a typical eastern Scottish river this is also the time at which the spring snow-melt gives out, and the river now becomes dependent upon rainfall and the run-off of rainwater to keep its levels up and its flow fresh. All too often the rain fails, and the late springs and early summers of many years in the 1970s and 1980s were characterised by prolonged periods of little or no rainfall in the salmon river catchments. Water levels drop steadily when these conditions persist, the temperature of the water rises in response to days and weeks of warm and sunny weather, and warm water contains less dissolved oxygen than cold water. The fish are affected by the reduced oxygen levels and tend to concentrate wherever fresher, better oxygenated water is to be found. Waterfalls and areas of bubbling broken water help to invest the river water with a higher oxygen level, and for this reason salmon will often congregate below falls and immediately downstream of white water stretches. For this reason the warm-weather, low-water flyfisher will pay especial attention to the heads of the pools, where falling water or fast, bubbling flows gradually lead in to the main body of the pool. There many of the fish will lie, preferring that refreshed and re-oxygenated water to the conditions elsewhere, and some will also retreat into the cooler and better oxygenated depths of the deepest and shadiest pools.

Chapter 10   Casting a Fly

This is not a book about flycasting. Indeed, the ability to cast a fly well, with accuracy and to considerable distances, despite adverse winds and physical obstacles such as high banks and overhanging trees, can sometimes be regarded as a distinct achievement, and quite separate from the successful catching of fish. Tournament casting is a sport in its own right, and the best practitioners can achieve miracles of distance and accuracy which are awesome to watch. Many experts, especially in the USA, concentrate on winning prizes at competitions and angling fairs, and seldom or never simply go out and try to apply their casting abilities to the catching of a fish. Others, despite their remarkable practical casting skills, never manage to catch salmon consistently, usually because they have neglected to cultivate the other arts which are necessary for success.

A moderate or even rather poor caster who is nevertheless skilled at reading the water, and at presenting and fishing a fly, will always catch more salmon than a brilliant caster who gives little or no thought to reading the water, or to where or how his fly is fishing. Competence at casting is therefore only one of several skills the salmon flyfisher must acquire. It is, as logicians would say, a necessary but not a sufficient precondition for consistent success. And if I were a salmon, the very last person I would want to find fishing down my pool is the chap who can not only cast a good line under all conditions but then proceeds to work down the water with thoughtfully applied skill, perhaps covering a stretch repeatedly with different sizes of fly fished at different speeds and depths, without alarming me or disturbing me in my lie – until he presents the one lure whose shape and movement I simply find irresistible! He is the sort of omnicompetent flyfisher who is most likely to trigger a fish's taking response and end the day with a salmon or two on the grass when other, less widely skilled fishers may have a blank, even though their casting may have been impeccable all day long.

Casting skills are best learned by good example and skilled tuition, either under the guidance of an adept friend or – usually much better – as the pupil of a qualified instructor. Many skilled individuals in all kinds of physical sports can perform brilliantly but are simply unable to explain quite how they do it, or to teach others to do so. To watch an expert caster in action, like any skilled craftsman, is to witness effortless competence which looks so easy, yet which can be so maddeningly elusive when the beginner tries to do it himself. The best way forward is to watch and learn from someone who can both demonstrate and teach, and the soundest grounding for any flyfisher is to take at least a few lessons from a good casting coach. The Association of Professional Game Angling Instructors (APGAI) maintains a network of accredited instructors throughout Britain and Ireland, and many of their members advertise regularly in the fishing magazines. Your tackle shop will almost certainly be able to put you in touch with a local member of the Association. Lessons are cheap if they put your feet on the right path for decade of successful fishing.

A capable instructor can teach by both precept and example, can analyse a beginners' defects of technique and correct them, and can show his pupil how and why the various casting techniques work. In time the pupil's own casting will become a matter of effortless second nature, but those lessons will have established a grounding of good technique and sound understanding. Then, on those occasional days when your timing and rhythm mysteriously desert you, when the line collapses in a heap at your feet or gets hung up incessantly in trees, you can go back to those first principles you learned and begin to correct your own faults. Shooters, tennis players and golfers all do the same on their off-days, provided good tuition has created that vital basis of understanding and sound fundamental technique. The self-taught "natural" caster has no such helpful basis to fall back upon when he hits a bad patch, as most do from time to time.

A few lessons lasting no more than an hour or so each will establish the basics of good casting, not only in the straightforward overhead style but also in other modes such as the roll cast and the double- and single-Spey casts. Practice and more practice, with an occasional formal lesson as a refresher, will gradually make perfect. And other aids are useful, especially some of the excellent flycasting video films which are now readily available. Although you may not have a rod in your hands, you can at least watch and listen as a capable instructor demonstrates the various styles of casting – a useful way of passing the time, and very pleasant too on a winter's evening when the rods are stored away for the close season. A video cassette costing £25-£30 may soon pay for itself in terms of casting satisfaction and fish on the bank, especially if it is shared among a few friends or by fellow members of a fishing club.

Books on fly casting are, with very few exceptions, generally unsatisfactory. They attempt in halting words and static pictures to convey the essence of activities which are fundamentally dynamic, fluent and rhythmic. A notable exception to this general judgement is Peter Mackenzie-Philps' outstanding *Flycasting Handbook*, which can be highly recommended for all flyfishers, novices and old hands alike. It is unrivalled for the clarity of its explanations and the instructive quality of its photographs, and shows a wide range of basic, advanced and specialised

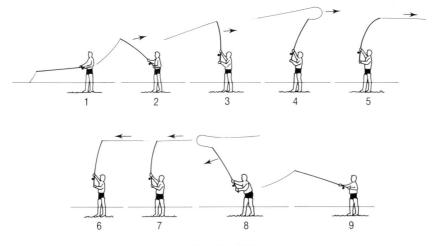

The Overhead Cast.

casting techniques for single- and double-handed rods – a most useful addition to your bookshelves, and a valuable adjunct to practical tuition under the watchful tutelage of a good instructor.

The overhead cast, at least in its single-handed form, will be familiar to all trout flyfishers and is the most commonly used casting method in British flyfishing. It is less universally used in salmon flyfishing, for reasons which will soon become apparent, but every salmon flyfisher should be familiar with it and capable of casting well in the overhead mode with both single- and double-handed rods. It is not the style you will necessarily prefer for most of your river flyfishing for salmon, and you may find you eventually almost abandon it, but it remains the only way of casting an ultra-heavy sinking or shooting-head flyline, for example.

The other techniques which are essential skills for consistently successful salmon fishing are the roll cast and both types of Spey cast. The roll cast is important not only as a means of pushing out a straight line when clearance behind the flyfisher is limited, but also for raising a sunken line to the surface as a preliminary to making a fresh cast at a different angle. Only a fully floating line can be flicked back and aerialised effectively for a new forward cast all in one go. Intermediate and sinking lines must first be rolled up to the surface before the back-cast plucks them off the water and into the air for a fresh cast.

The Spey casts have a great many advantages, and are really essential for effective and pleasureable river salmon fishing. They take their names from casting styles developed on the River Spey, where the banks tend to be high and much of the river is overhung with trees, both of which cause problems for anyone who relies on overhead casting. The essence of both types of Spey cast is that the vital springy casting power of the rod is brought into

A brace of silvery spring salmon. The exceptional beauty and superb sporting qualities of spring salmon make these the most highly prized fish of the salmon flyfisher's year.

Wading the Bank Pool of the Upper Beauly. A proven taking place for salmon is at the apex of the dark vee in the stream.

Sandy Leventon fishing shirtless in hot weather, on the Cork Blackwater in Ireland. This river is noted for its prolific runs of summer grilse and small salmon.

The River Orchy in high summer. Salmon lie in the well oxygenated broken water, and may come to flies fished by dibbling with a short line.

Clear water conditions in August on the River Findhorn. Salmon lie in narrow channels, and a long line cannot be closely controlled. Note how this flyfisher's light-coloured clothing assists camouflage among the pale rocky surroundings.

Gus McGonigle with a 7lb summer salmon from the River Erne in Co. Fermanagh, with Belleek's famous porcelain factory in the background. The Erne river and lough system is steadily improving as a summer salmon fishery, and costs are very moderate.

Tricky wading for Lavender Buckland on Perthshire's River Earn. It is often necessary to move up onto the bank for several casts before resuming in the water.

An end-of-season cock salmon from the Gledfield beat of the River Carron, above Bonar Bridge. Note its dark pre-mating coloration and prominent hooked kype.

ght trout tackle produced the only grilse of
is warm summer day, in low water
nditions on Sutherland's River Halladale.

Success on the loch! A fine silvery fish taken
on fly tackle.

A superb morning's harvest of fly-caught grilse and small summer salmon from the Ridge Pool on Co. Mayo's River Moy, probably Ireland's most prolific salmon river.

Salmon flies through the centuries – a wide range of styles and designs.

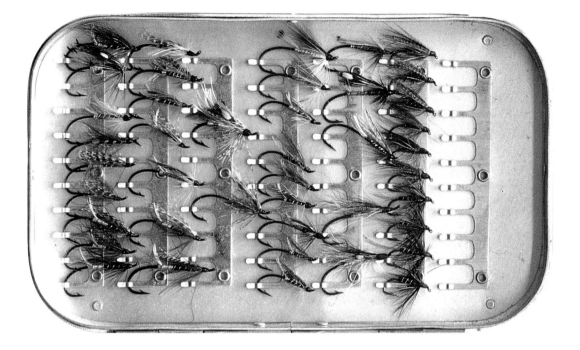

A selection of summer salmon flies, dressed on light single hooks.

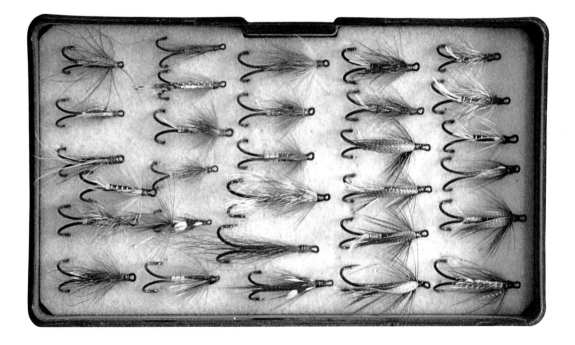

Summer salmon and grilse flies of various patterns, dressed on double hooks.

A grilse apiece, on the Upper Beauly.

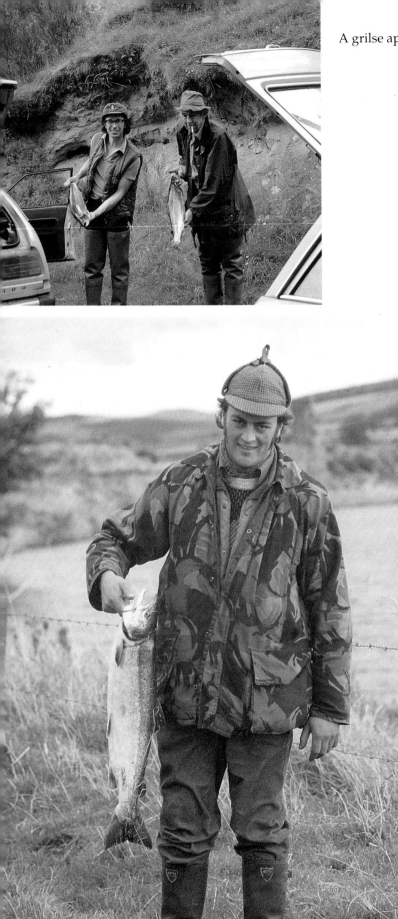

A nice late-season grilse for Tommy Hearn on the River Teviot, a Tweed tributary.

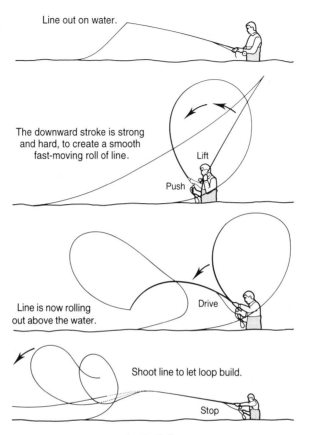

Line out on water.

The downward stroke is strong
and hard, to create a smooth
fast-moving roll of line.

Lift

Push

Line is now rolling
out above the water.

Drive

Shoot line to let loop build.

Stop

The Roll Cast.

play by the resistance of a carefully manipulated loop or roll of flyline on
the water, to one side of the angler or in front of him, instead of relying
solely upon the weight of a length of line in the air to load the spring in the
rod. The Spey casts dispense with any need to throw a long length of line
behind, and this is an obvious advantage where high banks and nearby trees
lurk in wait to ensnare your fly and leader, and then to expend your time
and temper in constantly retrieving and unravelling them. Especially when
the angler is wading some way out in the river, the appropriate type of Spey
cast can allow even a very long line to be put out neatly and accurately
without the line or the fly passing to his rear. Many wonderfully productive
pools, and some whole beats on certain rivers, are virtually unfishable for
those who cannot Spey-cast.

There is a further very important safety bonus, in that a single or double
Spey cast can be used, as appropriate, to keep the fly well clear of the
fisher's body at all times, especially when a strong wind is blowing. The
single Spey will keep a fast-moving, sharp and possibly heavy fly well away

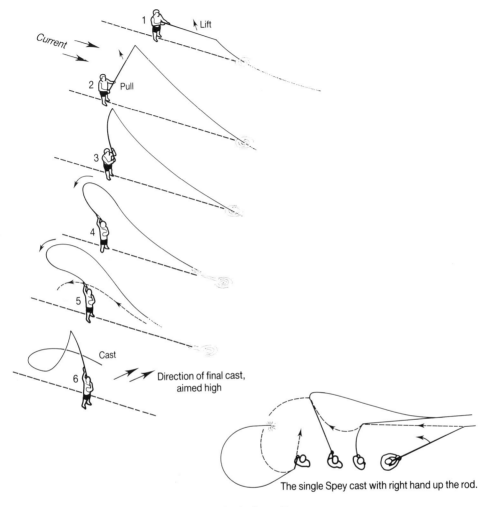

The Single Spey Cast.

from your vulnerable eyes and ears when there is a stiff upstream wind, and the double Spey will do the same when there is a strong downstream blow. Any salmon fly, even a tiny single hook, can do dreadful damage, or at the very least be a thorough nuisance, when it hits exposed flesh or even your outer clothing when it is travelling at the very high speed generated by most casting. And it needs little imagination to picture the harm that may be done by a heavy 3-inch brass or copper tube fly armed with a needle-sharp treble hook and travelling at speeds approaching 100 miles an hour, if it should chance to hit an eye, an earlobe or any flesh. Even through several layers of thick clothing such a missile can cause a painful blow and leave a nasty bruise. One or other of the Spey casts, chosen according to the conditions, will avoid all such problems and risks.

Mastery of this basic repertoire of four casts – overhead, roll, single and double Spey – will enable any flyfisher to tackle almost any salmon fishing situation with some confidence and in comfort, and both of these are very conducive to success. (Dapping, a fifth form of putting out a fly over a fish, is dependent upon wind assistance and thus cannot really be included in a list of active casting styles, and it is discussed elsewhere, in the section on loch fishing for salmon.)

Finally, there is the additional pleasure of simply being able to cast well. Even when the river seems fishless and dead, there is a great deal of sensory – almost sensual – pleasure to be derived from the execution of a good cast. The Spey casts in particular have a unique combination of rhythm and economy of movement which makes them look and feel like piscatorial poetry in motion.

The casting ends and fishing the fly really begins in earnest when the cast is complete and the line, leader and fly are all in or on the water, although a great deal depends on the way in which the cast has been executed to ensure that the fly is presented as desired, and begins to behave as it should as soon as possible after it lands in the water.

All flyfishing, of whatever kind, involves the angler's deliberate use or avoidance of drag, and the salmon flyfisher needs to have a clear idea of how he wishes his line, leader and fly to behave in relation to the movement of the water. To let the fly move downstream as though it were simply an object carried on or in the current, like a leaf or a twig – usually referred to as a "dead drift" – is unusual and seldom required in European salmon flyfishing, but it can only be achieved if the fisher is able to cast and then manipulate his line so as to eliminate all lateral dragging of the fly caused by the force of the river current or the breeze bearing upon the line, and this is usually best achieved by making a slack cast, to avoid any tension in the line which may be transmitted through the leader to the fly, thereby affecting its movement on or through the water.

Much more typical than dead-drifting, however, is the salmon flyfisher's need to recognise that the flow of the water and the force of the wind exert pressures upon the line and leader, and then be able to manipulate his tackle so as to regulate these forces and make use of them to cause the fly to move in the desired way. For the practised flyfisher the cast is only the beginning of a continuum of movement, that first extends the line, leader and fly upon the water and then modulates and controls their position, speed and depth. Good casting is therefore not only the initial means whereby the fly is launched into the desired position; it is also critical for the skilful control of the fly's movement until a fresh cast is made and the procedure begins afresh.

Chapter 11　Reconnaissance

"Time spent in reconnaissance is never wasted". The soldier's adage can equally well be applied to the battle of wits and skill in which the salmon flyfisher contends with his quarry. The natural eagerness to put the rod up immediately and get down quickly to the river or onto the loch should be firmly resisted and energies channelled into fruitful preparation. Assuming you have planned to take a week's fishing holiday, or to rent a salmon beat for a period – and this is usually done by the week – the first preparatory step is to acquire good maps and plans of the general area and of the particular beat you are intending to fish. Make sure that these are as detailed and up to date as possible, and then pore over them with great care. This is not only a valuable preliminary to successful fishing: it is also a pleasantly anticipatory activity in its own right, like sipping an aperitif and enjoying the delicious smells emanating from the kitchen before you get down to the main meal in earnest.

Go through the maps and river plans carefully, making mental and perhaps written notes as you do so. Refer also to any mentions of your river, or, even better, your particular beat, which may occur in the standard reference books such as Mills & Graesser's definitive *The Salmon Rivers of Scotland*, John Ashley-Cooper's *The Great Salmon Rivers of Scotland*, or Peter O'Reilly's comprehensive two volumes on Ireland's salmon and trout waters. Check also the valuable fisheries' reports published monthly in magazines such as *Trout & Salmon*. Individual beats and stretches are often mentioned there, and all this information helps to build up a valuable mental picture of the water before you actually set eyes on it.

A good contour map, such as the excellent Ordnance Survey 1:50,000 series (just over one inch to the mile) and, even better, the 1:25,000 and 1:10,000 series, can enable you to build up a highly detailed impression of the lie of the land and to make some educated assumptions about such matters as the orientation of the river and thus of the angles of direct sunshine at various times during a bright fishing day. The position of fishing huts, car parking places, pedestrian access points and rights of way should also be identified and noted in advance of your arrival, all of which helps to familiarise you in advance – and it is also a very pleasant form of armchair sport in its own right.

When your fishing holiday actually begins, leave home in good time and arrive well before the beginning of your fishing lease. Most changeovers take place on Sundays, especially in Scotland, where salmon fishing is not legal on the Sabbath. Sunday is therefore a good day to go and have a thorough look at the river, not a cursory glance through the window of your car as you drive by, but a careful and critical inspection on foot. This is the fisher's equivalent of a jockey walking the course, to inspect the jumps and get a feel for what lies ahead.

On reaching the river, check the boundaries (called "marches" in Scotland) and the individual names and sequence of the pools, and all the other details you have noted, against the map and your earlier notes. Much of what you find will be as you have anticipated, but some details may be unexpected. Estate cottages and fishing huts can be built or demolished almost overnight, whole woods of commercial conifers can be clear-felled in a matter of weeks, and new features of the landscape and the river topography may then have to be taken into account. Spate rivers where heavy winter flooding occurs may be completely reshaped during the close season by the force of the water, as it sculpts new pools out of the shifting boulders and gravel. Remember that no map, however good, is ever quite up to date. And the very best maps and plans are likely to be in the estate office or the fishery office, so that will amply repay a visit. There you will probably have a chance to introduce yourself to the agent (or factor, in Scotland), to get chatting about the fishing, and to discover where and when you can meet the water keeper, the gillie, the boatman or some of the local fishers, all of whose brains are well worth picking over a companionable dram before your fishing begins. Get a map of the beat you will be fishing, if the office can supply copies; and if not, try asking them to photocopy their master map for you.

Locate the water gauge, if there is one, as this will be an important barometer to which you will find you refer constantly throughout your stay. On well maintained beats the gauge usually consists of a wide plank or board painted in black and white, on which the water height can readily be told by reference to a clearly marked calibration in feet and inches. The gauge is often placed fairly conspicuously, within sight of a bridge or a car parking place, so you can read it instantly before you even get down to the waterside. If there is not a gauge, or if the beat is a long one with only one gauge, place a twig or stick in the sand or gravel at the water's edge on your arrival, and refer to it constantly. Salmon behaviour and movements are often significantly affected by even quite small changes in water height, and you will want to be aware of these and adjust your tackle and tactics accordingly. The locals, including the fishery owner and the gillie, may well rely on familiar rocks and boulders to calculate the state of the river, which is all very well for them. But a newcomer may find it more difficult to identify that particular rock among all the hundreds of others. Stick to watching the gauge, however makeshift.

It is well worth going through all of this preliminary reconnaissance every time you revisit a favourite stretch of river, especially if your visits are confined to only one week each year. You may well find there have been considerable changes since your last visit, thanks to the combined forces of man and nature. Fences and stiles may have been replaced or repositioned, the shape and size of some pools may have been significantly altered by the erosion of winter storm-water, and a fallen tree or a collapsed length of bank can make a big difference to a well known pool and how it is best fished. These latter factors can be important on some of the wilder and more remote salmon waters of Britain and Ireland, where riparian maintenance can sometimes be rather haphazard, and sometimes nonexistent.

Most of the Rods who have been fishing your water during the preceding week will probably begin their journeys home on Sunday morning, and you are therefore unlikely to have any worthwhile opportunity of talking to them unless you arrive on the previous evening. It is well worth doing this, even though it will entail paying for an additional night's accommodation. These departing Rods will have the very hottest intelligence, having spent the last week fishing the selfsame pools that you will shortly be facing. It will usually not be difficult to locate them, and the chances are you may all be staying at the one and only fishing pub for miles around, so it is easy to contrive a meeting.

If you arrive not too late on the Saturday, you may even bump into the outgoing Rods on the riverbank. Never barge in upon strangers who are enjoying their final few hours on the river, and do nothing to distract any Rod who is actually intent upon fishing. By all means introduce yourself to any Rod who happens to be taking a rest, but remember that privacy and peace are important parts of what you pay for when you rent a salmon beat. It is not unreasonable to expect to be left alone to enjoy them without interruption. You may, of course, meet a hospitable party who will warmly invite you to share the contents of their flasks in the hut at teatime, but do not take it for granted. If perchance they have had a bleak and fishless week they may not be in a particularly good humour.

With a few disagreeable exceptions, however, fishers are a sociable lot, and you are likely to find your predecessors only too glad to spill out an account of their triumphs and disasters over a cup of tea or a drink on their last evening. If you can find a quiet corner in the residents' lounge or the bar, spread out a map on the table and go over their week's sport with them. The results may make a considerable difference to the extent of your own success or failure, and the cost of a round of drinks is a small price to pay for it.

While the out-going tenants are sure to be an excellent potential source of intelligence, the gillie is by far the best informant of all. After all, he spends his working life on that stretch of water, seeing it in all its moods, and his knowledge is therefore priceless. Many Highland gillies are taciturn and reserved by nature, sparing with words, and sometimes a little uncertain of strangers for the first few hours on the river, until they have had time to size you up. But if you can track down your gillie before you start your week's fishing, and can impress him with your genuine enthusiasm and interest, he may gradually reveal information that will greatly enhance your pleasure and chances of success, right from the outset. Buy him a dram, spread out a map of the beat, and let him guide you through it. A mass of questions will come into your mind. Why is that oddly-named pool so-called? What are the best pools with the water at this height? Which ones will be improved by higher, or lower, water levels? Where is deep wading necessary? Are the lies deep, calling for a well-sunk fly? What styles and sizes of flies does he recommend? Where does he propose to start you and your companions off on Monday morning? How long should it take to fish such-and-such a pool? His answers to these and countless other questions will help you to build up a continually improving mental picture of what to expect and what tactics to adopt; and it is worth covering that map with pencilled notes for further study.

Finally, before you put out the bedside light and start to dream of salmon, listen to the late-night local weather forecast. The promise of hotter or colder weather may influence tomorrow's fishing, and the likelihood of rain is especially important. Remember, too, that it is not the rain falling overhead that will affect your beat and your fishing, but the rainfall many miles upstream. But remember, too, that weather forecasts can often be very wide of the mark, especially in the wilder northern and western parts of Britain. Not only do the forecasters tend to concentrate on the more populous southern regions; they are also largely powerless to predict the erratic weather patterns in mountainous countryside, where the conditions in one glen or valley may be quite different from those just a few miles away over the hills in the next river catchment.

Next morning, do not feel you have to rise with the lark. But do not delay either, and make sure that all your tackle is ready for prompt assembly. Too many people are prepared to have a slow and faltering start to their first day's fishing, and regard the first couple of hours as a time for gradually getting themselves, their clothing and tackle organised. By contrast, a well-prepared angler may have put in almost half a day's serious fishing while all this unnecessary fumbling has been going on, and may even have opened the score with a fish or two. A fishing party, like any sporting group, goes at the pace of the slowest member, so try to ensure that you are all equally well prepared and do not keep one another hanging around unnecessarily.

The gillie will, as always, politely wait for even the slowest member to get ready, but he will be very much happier if you do not keep him waiting. After all, you have probably had weeks of anticipation in which to sort out, prepare and pack all your tackle, which should all be ready for swift assembly. Even if you are on your own, or just fishing with a friend and without the guidance of a gillie, there is no point in wasting time unnecessarily sorting out gear that could have been prepared the night before. You are here to fish, and not to dawdle over tasks that should have been sorted out yesterday, or perhaps weeks ago!

Your approach to the river, or the loch, should be a carefully considered one. Trout fishermen are accustomed to going cautiously, conscious of how easy it is to alarm fish and put down those that are feeding. It may be less obvious with salmon, which are very unlikely to be feeding on the surface like trout, but they have eyes, too, and sensitive lateral-line nerve systems for detecting vibrations. It is crazy to clump incautiously down to the water's edge, or (worse) to stride the length of the pool with your shadow falling heavily across the water that you intend to start fishing.

Approach gently, keep a low profile, and try not to cast a shadow ahead of you across or down the pool. Part of your pre-fishing reconnaissance should have been to work out the orientation of the pools and the beat in general, so that you can take into account the position and angle of the sun in advance. If you cast a long and sombre shadow it is potentially very frightening to the fish; the sun in your eyes or glittering off the water ahead of you makes it more difficult to watch your line and monitor the way the fly is fishing; and if bright sunshine is falling on the water you may choose to use a quite different size and colour of fly than if the same stretch of water were in the shade.

The traditional way to fish fly-water of the classic type is to start at the head of a pool and fish it down steadily, ending at the tail. But this general observation must take account of the nature of the water, both in terms of the shape and layout of the pool, and also the relative height and speed of the water. Salmon will behave differently with varying circumstances of water height, speed and clarity, and will often choose to lie in quite different areas of the pool as the conditions change. This is the kind of expert local knowledge that gillies, owners and regular Rods build up over successive seasons, and the really diligent ones may go as far as to make up a fishery map to indicate where fish tend to lie under varying circumstances. One of the cleverest ways of doing this is by means of a series of sheets of greaseproof paper or opaque acetate that overlie one another, each sheet indicating the likely lies of salmon for a particular height of water in the pool. It is amusing and often very instructive to make up one of these fish maps, based on your experience of fishing a beat regularly over a number of seasons, and perhaps doing so in co-operation with fishing friends, other tenants and the gillie. If only more fishery owners and their gillies would prepare these little guides, it would be much appreciated by their tenants. But the resident gillie will have the mental equivalent of such a series of maps, which is why his guidance is so very valuable.

As a broad generalisation, medium to low water levels in a river will tend to cause salmon to lie in the streamier and better oxygenated portions of a pool, especially from late spring onwards, when the warmer water holds a lower amount of dissolved oxygen than the chill waters of the early part of the season. In summer, fish that have moved upstream in the night, both salmon and seatrout, will often be found to have taken up station by the side of streamy, bubbling water, and, quite typically, just below the heads of the pools if there is a brisk and tumbling flow of water at those points. Colder water, and a minor spate or freshet at any time of year, may cause fish in the same pools to linger close in by the banks and out of the main power of the current, or in the slacker waters at the tails of the pools. The prevailing conditions will largely dictate your approach, and if your first cast of the day is on a pool that is warm and on the low side, you will often find yourself beginning well above the head of the pool, casting down into any throats of white water, and concentrating your first and best efforts on the lively, oxygen-rich areas of the pools. In high water, or when the river is dropping and clearing after a flood, you will probably spend an equal amount of time concentrating upon the slacker stretches, the sheltered lies and the tails of the pools, where salmon may be resting after ascending from lower parts of the river.

While the traditional approach is to fish a pool downstream from head to tail, there are times and conditions which will dictate the very reverse of this. A long, deep, slow-flowing stretch, for example, may offer little or no opportunity to work a fly down and across with the assistance of the current in making the fly move, in which case you may have to hand-line or strip in your fly to give it the motion and appearance of life that the force of the current usually contributes. A highly effective technique, that deserves to me more widely known and used, is called backing-up. In its purest form this involves beginning at the tail of the pool, where you cast more or less directly across the river at right angles to the current, and then take two or three brisk steps upstream. This has the effect of putting a prominent downstream belly in the line, causing the sluggish current to catch the curve of the line, rather as light airs catch the spinnaker of a yacht, and move the fly in a lively sweep across the pool. In especially dour and lifeless pools this can be further assisted by stripping in line by hand as you step upstream.

Not only does this tactic give a brisk animation to the fly in a way that conventional down-and-across fishing cannot; it also presents the fly to the fish in a different way. Often the first sight a lying salmon will get of the fly is as it flicks into sight from behind (i.e. from downstream), and this can sometimes trigger a decisive – even savage – take from a fish that would otherwise be moribund and unresponsive. The combination of the fish's energy in taking and the sideways movement of the backed-up fly across a pool means that a high proportion of fish taken this way are very firmly hooked on first contact.

By the same token, very low, clear water conditions, especially in summer and early autumn, may indicate an upstream approach, this time by casting well upstream and somewhat diagonally across the river, in a way that is rather reminiscent of upstream nymphing for trout. And, as in much trouting, you may also be able to see your fish clearly, lying ahead of you upstream. If you can see them, they will most definitely be able to see you, and a shadow or a bankside silhouette would probably be fatal, putting the fish on the alert and sending them fleeing. Instead, you cast upstream and across, with a floating line and a small fly, and bringing its bright and wake-creating shape across their window of view in a way that is as close as the British salmon flyfisher will normally get to genuine dry-fly fishing for salmon.

The final decisions about which tactics and tackle will be best to use are, of course, only made once you are at the water's edge, but reconnaissance and thoughtful planning go a long way towards successful fishing by preparing you mentally, and in terms of having the appropriate tackle ready to hand, for the business of getting down to some serious fishing.

Chapter 12   Flies for Salmon

The fly – or flies, for you will quite often fish with two on your leader – represents the sharp end of your equipment, for it is this, and only this, that you wish to salmon to see. By its combination of size, shape, colour and movement it will – if all goes well – succeed in deceiving a salmon into abandoning its non-feeding habits in freshwater and engulfing it, an act that may be a feeding response, or motivated by curiosity or aggression, or possibly some combination of these. The fly is therefore the most critical element in your armoury – assuming, of course, that all the rest of your tackle is up to scratch. There is no point in having the killing fly on your leader if you cannot present it to the fish in the correct place and manner, or in getting the fish to take it if you cannot then play him with the power, sensitivity and control that are necessary to bring him safely to hand.

Sizeable books have been written on the subject of salmon flies alone – I estimated about a dozen of them in print in Britain alone in 1994 – and more are sure to follow. The variety of flies, in size, shape and colour, is vast and continually growing, a trend which is given added impetus by the fact that many fly-dressers now enjoy devising new patterns purely as a creative aesthetic exercise. Salmon flies, especially in the older, fully-dressed styles and in many modern designs using new synthetic dressing materials, are highly decorative and artistic creations in their own right, and are often dressed with no intention that they should ever be used for the practical business of fishing. And as regards their practical value as fishing lures, any gathering of salmon fishers is almost guaranteed to slip into animated discussion of fly styles and patterns, while every gillie on every beat will have his own ideas about what are the best flies for that particular piece of water under various conditions. The flyfisher's scope for experimentation is almost boundless, and this richness and variety is one of the character-istically delightful aspects of the sport, that only a kill-joy would seek to suppress. Salmon flies are intrinsically fascinating objects, and form an absorbing topic in their own right. The lovely confections of feather, hair and tinsel displayed in every tackle shop are clearly successful in catching salmon fisherman, and most of them, used under the appropriate circumstances, will also catch salmon.

So what are the principles in choosing a fly that will actually catch a fish? Can we identify any essential qualities that comprise a successful fly for salmon? First, we must beware of taking the term fly too literally. With a few rare exceptions, salmon flies are not intended to be representations of any known insect, and only in a few patterns are they constructed to look like a specific aquatic creature. Yes, salmon and grilse do occasionally rise to a mayfly imitation, and some well known patterns are intended to approximate in appearance to shrimps and prawns. But the term "lure" is really more appropriate for the vast majority of salmon flies, since that is their function – to catch the eye of a fish and lure or entice a salmon that does not ordinarily feed in freshwater into taking hold of it. But the term "lure" tends readily to be associated with spinning and trolling baits, and so, by tradition, we flyfishers are left with the conventional, if strictly inaccurate, term "fly".

First, the fly must be constructed in a way that gives it an appropriate shape when it is in the water, and intimately allied to its shape is the second criterion, movement. Both shape and movement are products of the materials the fly-dresser uses, and of the way in which those materials behave when the fly is in the water. That fly in your box, which, when dry, looks so full-bodied and well-feathered, will assume a wholly different appearance when it is wetted and immersed in water, especially flowing water. In the water, most flies are designed to assume a shape which, to the salmon, is suggestive of some other credible form of aquatic life – a small fish, perhaps, or a sand-eel, or a crustacean. The common factor in virtually all of these is a more or less streamlined and sleek outline, such as can be seen in most creatures that live and move about in water. The long shanks of the typical hooks, or tubes and hooks, or mounts and hooks used for tying a salmon fly, allow the dresser to apply materials so as to create this desirably slender and elongated profile, particularly when the fly is in motion in the water. Many salmon patterns look ample and bushy – some almost plump – when they are taken dry out of your fly box, but once they are wet they assume a very much slimmer and more attenuated shape, and therefore give a quite different impression.

To the fly's shape must be allied a measure of movement in the water, for it is the combination of shape and animation that together give an impression of life and activity. Tinsels and wires help to form the shape and etch the outlines of a fly's pattern, but it is the softer materials such as hair, feathers, fur and wool that move in response to tiny variations in the flow and pressure of the water upon them, or, in the case of flies used for stillwater fishing in lochs, by the pluck of the line in concert with the action of the wind and the waves. These soft and mobile parts of the structure are the elements in the fly's dressing that convey a sense of independent life, moving in subtle and effortless ways that are strongly suggestive of flickering fins and waving tails and feelers. As the strands and tufts and wings of these soft materials move in the water, they not only create an impression of animation and activity by their own movements, but by the way in which they reveal and cover and reveal again the harder bodily outlines formed by the underlying wrappings of wires and tinsels, and the wools and hair applied in creating the body. Even if seen in monochrome, as on a black and white movie film, the wavings and pulsatings of the feathers and hair and fur create the impression of flashing and glittering from the underlying shiny elements of the fly's dressing.

Thirdly comes colour, and this is perhaps the most contentious and endlessly discussed aspect of fly design, not only among salmon anglers but in the more directly imitative sphere of the trout flyfisher's activities. Does colour matter? Can salmon see in colour? And if so, what colours best replicate those of their natural food species, or of other creatures that might stimulate either curiosity or aggression? And how is colour related to the size, shape and movement of the fly, and to the changing clarity of the water and the ambient light?

Lengthy discussion of the successful shapes, styles and colours of salmon flies has filled a good many books already, and will continue to do so; and anyone interested in exploring the infinitely varied world of salmon fly development can do no better than immerse himself in one or more of the specialised books on this subject, which are listed in the bibliography at the end of this book. In the context of this more general introduction to salmon flyfishing, however, there is only scope for a consideration of some basic principles.

Fashions in salmon fly theory come and go, but there has been a marked trend among British salmon fishers since the 1970s towards regarding the size and movement of the fly as the most critical elements in its success, with the overall impression of colour coming next, and the finer details of precise coloration or mixtures of colours coming rather low on their list of priorities. Perhaps the best word to sum it up is jizz – originally, the military observer's "general impression of size and shape" – which is the best term I know for summing up the way in which we, and most other creatures, see the world around us. The minutiae of anatomy, structure and coloration are not what we first look for in identifying an object, whether it is a living creature or something inanimate, and this is especially true if that object happens to be moving. We see and interpret retinal images in terms of their size, their shape, the way in which they move, and their degree of relative contrast with their surroundings. What matters are not the individual little component parts but the general impression of size, shape and movement created by the assembled package. For that reason I would slightly modify jizz by adding *am* for "and movement", and if the *jizzam* is convincing then the design, however it is achieved, has been successful.

At its simplest and most extreme, this theory of jizzam boils down to a very clear-cut philosophy of fly design, and some of the most consistently successful British salmon anglers of the 1990s have taken this approach towards its limits by resolving their selection of flies into a choice of only two basic colour types – light and dark – and a range of sizes within each of those colour groups. By doing this they have cut right through all the myriad complexities and variations that are so colourfully depicted in the illustrated encyclopedias of salmon flies, and at a stroke have swept away all hesitations and deliberations about the finer points of fly design, especially as regards coloration. Critics of this philosophy maintain that it lacks subtlety: its afficionados respond by saying that it eliminates what is irrelevant by focussing upon what really makes a killing fly. The proof of the pudding is in the eating, and many practitioners of the simplified system maintain very impressive success rates with salmon under all types of water conditions. Others of the more complex and varied school of fly selection and design seem to do equally well – which may merely demonstrate that it is confidence and perseverance that really count, along with skill in fly presentation and an ability to read the water accurately.

Trout flyfishers will probably be well aware of the widely quoted rule-of-thumb for choosing general fly coloration according to the weather conditions – "bright day, bright fly; dull day, dull fly". That broad guidance is largely followed by those salmon fishers who favour the two colours theory of fly pattern, and they will generally use the darker of their patterns in overcast or low light conditions, and the brighter style in sunshine or under a light sky. But in addition to the available light, the clarity of the water also comes into consideration here and modifies the eventual choice, so that a significant degree of colour in the river will indicate that a bright fly is preferable, even though it may be a generally dull day. Brightness and contrast make such a fly easier for the fish to see in water that is turbid and murky.

In addition to choosing a fly to match the prevailing weather and any colour in the water, another consideration involves the choice of a fly that will be in keeping with the river or loch environment in which it is to be used. In the temperate freshwaters of Britain and Ireland, and elsewhere in the Atlantic salmon's range, small fish and other aquatic creatures tend to be subtly and discreetly coloured, blending well into their surroundings, and not appearing too conspicuous – certainly never lurid or garish. Therefore, if our chosen salmon fly is intended to represent or echo the shape and movement of a natural creature, it should not be an exotically bright splash of vivid primary colours. Such beasties simply do not occur in our salmon rivers and lochs, and so the majority of fly patterns have a generally subtle and muted colour in the water, however bright and tinselly they may appear when dry and in their boxes. In waters that drain from peaty uplands and have a characteristic pale stain the colour of China tea, the more muted patterns tend to be the most used and the most consistently successful, while in rivers that flow over limestone and chalk the water is altogether clearer and often has a hint of steely blueness, and in such conditions flies with a greater degree of shimmer and an element of blue in the dressing often fare best.

However, because there are no such words as "always" and "never" in the vocabulary of the wise salmon flyfisher, these vaguely representational and colour-matched choices can sometimes fail to move fish when another pattern, altogether more lurid and bizarre, succeeds. A case in point occurred on the Findhorn in August, in conditions of extreme low water, when the rocky pools were full of seemingly stale and moribund salmon. The tenants fished with their utmost delicacy and skill with tiny Stoat's Tail flies, which were consistently ignored by the fish. Then the owner of the beat appeared, chatted and condoled with the anglers on their lack of sport, and proceeded to cast a bright yellow 3-inch Waddington square across the pool, fishing it back in a fast sweep down and across. On his second cast the fly was taken with savage energy, and ten minutes later the fish was duly landed. That fast-fished, large, ultra bright fly looked and behaved like no natural denizen of those waters, but something in its appearance and movement had broken the spell and induced a decisively vigorous take. So much for the conventional wisdom of tiny naturalistic flies in very low water!

The fly is attached to the leader at the eye, of course, which rather tends to make us conclude that the fish seizes the fly at the very end – i.e. at the hook. In fact, salmon and most other piscivorous and carnivorous fish attack and engulf their prey head first, and if a salmon takes your fly to represent some form of fish or other vertebrate creature, its usual approach will be to seize it head on. (Of course, there are exceptions, and one of the commonest is when a salmon follows a fly that is being slowly hand-lined in "on the dangle", in preparation for a fresh cast, when it may well be grabbed from directly astern – alas, often resulting only in a precarious lip-hold for the hook.) If a head-on or sideways angle of attack is the norm, the position of the hook or hooks in relation to the total length and structure of the fly can be varied. In the case of hairwing flies tied on low-water double hooks, the dressing may end well up the shank of the hook, with the remainder of the hook extending quite far behind the fly's body. Most patterns tied on Esmond Drury-type long-shanked treble hooks have the tips of the longest fibres of the dressing extending a little way beyond the hooks; while many patterns tied on tubes and in the Waddington style have as much as half the total length of the dressing extending to the rear of the hooks, and sometimes even more. The Collie Dog is probably the most extreme example of a dressing that extends far behind the hook, with its long wing of black collie's hair, perhaps 6-9 inches long, trailing far astern of the much shorter silvery tube body and its usual treble hook.

Discussion with a few fellow anglers will soon reveal that theories about the relative hook position can vary considerably, with some firmly expressing their preference for hooks set well to the rear of most dressings, on the basis that this may hook a fish that would otherwise "come short", simply plucking half-heartedly at the trailing ends of the dressing. It is interesting to note that this theory is particularly widespread among salmon anglers who are principally seatrout fishers, or whose flyfishing began with seatrout as the main quarry. Seatrout can be notoriously short takers, and many flies and lures for seatrout fishing are deliberately designed with extra trailing hooks or an additional little "flying treble" to overcome this problem. But salmon behave differently towards a fly, and it is interesting to note that most of the consistently successful and widely experienced salmon flyfishers have a preferences for flies dressed so that the wings and tail hairs extend well beyond the body of the fly, whether it is tied on a tube or a long-shanked treble. A ¼-inch tube fly may therefore have an overall length from the eye to the tips of the trailing hairs of perhaps an inch or more, while a 4-inch tube or Waddington-type fly may have a tube or hook length of only 2 inches or even a little less. This means the hook is closer to the point of seizure if the salmon takes the fly head-on, or even sideways, while the hook is partially concealed within the dressing of the fly, and the trailing strands of hair have maximum freedom to sway and pulsate in response to the movement of the water and the tension of the line, giving that illusion of animated life that is so important for the fly's success.

Fishing the Fly

A salmon fly – which, as we have seen, is essentially a lure intended by a combination of appearance and movement to entice the fish to attack it out of curiosity, aggression or a resurgence of its latent but suppressed feeding instincts – can only work if it has movement in the water. This essential movement can be imparted by the flow of the water, or by the flyfisher's manipulation of his rod and line, or by the action of the wind and waves as they catch the line and the leader, or by a combination of some or all of these.

The speed of the fly's movement is not an absolute matter: it must be considered in relation to the independent movements of water and wind, and in relation to the fish which it is intended to entice. A few salmon, only a tiny handful each season, are taken on floating flies fished on the top of the water and presented with a complete absence of the unnatural looking drag that scares off a feeding trout. It is for trout that almost all such flies are cast, at least in the British Isles and Europe, unlike the dry-fly tactics that can be so effective for salmon in the eastern seaboard rivers of north America, of which Lee Wulff has always been the chief and almost legendary exponent.

Dapping or dibbling, which involves using either the wind or the dipping and raising of the rod's tip, or the flow of a river's waters, or a combination of all of these, to impart a dipping, lifting, fluttering, skating and generally animated movement to a bushily dressed floating fly fished on the surface, or in the surface film, is an applied variant of the static, no-drag dry-fly method. It can be used on a river pool, or on the twirling waters that bubble below a waterfall or a section of white water, or tripped over the waves on a loch, from a boat drifting over known salmon lies.

But most flyfishing for salmon takes place on rivers, where the water's flow supplies a dynamic energy that can readily be used to impart movement and apparent life to an artificial fly. If you take a fly on its own and simply flick it out over the waters of a river or a loch, it will either promptly sink and be drawn away under the surface by the flow of the water; or else, if it is sufficiently buoyant, it will float and be wholly at the mercy of the current, the waves and the wind. In any event, it is unlikely to be of interest to a salmon. But attach it to the end of a flyline and leader, and that restraint immediately applies another force. Acting at an angle against the flow of the water, or the fly's tendency to sink, or the force of the breeze, the pull of the leader and line and rod exert a whole new influence upon the fly and how it behaves.

Herein lies the whole secret of the successful salmon flyfisher's art, using the combination of the resistance of the line and the rod, the action of current, wind and waves upon the line, and the angler's calculated manipulation of the rod and line to make the fly behave in the way he desires. It is the ability to judge and regulate the fly's movement, allied to an understanding of how the fly should best be worked to attract a fish under those circumstances, that makes the successful salmon fisher.

The three essential components in this matter of fly presentation involve the size of the fly, the depth at which it should be fished, and the speed at which it should be made to move relative to any resting, static salmon in the water being covered. Water temperature affects not only the behaviour of the salmon but of all other forms of life in the river, including potential food species, which is what the fly is intended to represent. In cold water conditions, a small fly that resembles a little fish and somehow appears to be able to move quickly against the river's flow will look unnatural to a salmon, itself torpid and sluggish in the chill water. Much more credible is a much larger artificial representation such as a long-winged fly of the Collie Dog type, for a fish of that size could be capable of comparatively rapid and energetic movement in cold water.

In addition to the impression that the fly and its size and movement make upon the watching salmon, there is the question of their proximity. A sluggish, torpid salmon lying deep in a pool has its liveliness suppressed by the cold, and is conserving its reserves of energy. It is therefore unlikely to move far or fast from its lie to attack a passing fly, especially one that is quite high in the water and some way off, whereas a more enlivened fish in the warmer waters of late spring and summer might be disposed to lunge powerfully at a fly passing many yards away. Furthermore, the fish of late spring or summer may be lying in much shallower water, so that a fly fished anywhere from the surface down to mid-water is much more likely to pass relatively close to it.

The challenge therefore is to present the fly to the lying fish in such a way as to make it both tempting and takeable. This helps to put into perspective the old, generalised rules-of-thumb that a cold-water fly should be small and fished briskly and high in the water, using a floating line. Large fly or small, sinking line or floater, the real challenge is to get the fly fishing close to the lying fish, with a movement that is appropriate to the water temperature and to the size of the fly in relation to the speed of the current.

The same general principles apply to flyfishing for salmon in the still waters of lochs, an undeservedly neglected aspect of gamefishing which nevertheless accounts for a great deal of sport in northern and western parts of the British Isles, and which is dealt with in some detail elsewhere in this book.

A medium or fast sinking line will take any size of fly well down into the depths, and the angler's ability to cast, mend and control the line will determine the speed at which the fly moves, relative to the lying fish and the speed of the flowing water. A fully floating line can also be used to fish a fly quite deeply, if it has weight and is at the end of a longish leader. But the combination of a floating line and a heavy, deep-fishing fly is usually an awkward one, since the fly is likely to move with an unnaturally nose-up attitude, instead of an even keel. Even in warmish waters with small, light flies, many experienced salmon flyfishers will opt to use an intermediate or slow-sinking line to present the fly at a balanced and level posture across the fishes' gaze.

The flow of the water – or, as we shall see, the movement of the waves and the pluck of the wind on the line in loch flyfishing – provides the force that is translated into a realistic speed and movement of the fly, if the flyfisher is attentive and skilled in managing the fishing-out of the cast. Flowing water on a river beat is a two-edged sword, which provides a source of motive power for the fly and can also move it in quite undesirable ways, if compensating manipulation of the flyline is not carefully applied.

Imagine, for example, a fairly typical stretch of water on a moderately wide river. It is quite easy for the angler to cast a good 25-30 yards square across the current, landing his fly in the rather slower flowing water towards the farther bank, while the line beneath his rod tip droops into an equally slow flow under his own bank. The bulk of his line lies out across the main stream of the current, which is considerable faster than the flows close under both banks. If it is left to follow the natural flow, the flyline is swiftly bent into a large downstream belly, as the fast flow of the main current catches and carries the line off with it. The effect of this belly is to exert tension on the far end of the line, with the leader and fly attached, causing the fly to be dragged swiftly downstream and across, at perhaps twice the speed of the main current, eventually to whip into line downstream of the main bulk of the flyline, slowing down as it does so, and eventually coming to rest in a dangling position downstream of the flyfisher as his line lies directly extended down the river.

This is obviously undesirable, because the comparatively bulky and visible floating flyline will sweep downstream well ahead of the fly, probably frightening any fish that are lying there, and its progress will be followed by the unnaturally fast-moving fly that will give the impression of something racing rapidly downstream. Instead, the object is to manipulate the line and the fly in such a way that the fly precedes the main flyline by as large a margin as the leader allows, while moving in a way that is realistic and credible to the watching salmon. This can only be achieved by careful and repeated manipulation of the flyline after the cast has been made, and throughout the course of the fly's downstream progress – a process known as mending the cast. The word mending here does not imply any kind of physical repair, but rather a series of movements of the rod and line that amend or improve the line's position and the effects of the current upon it, and thus upon the movement of the fly.

Instead of the scene just described, with the current taking the line off in a mid-stream belly and whipping the fly rapidly downstream, we aim to mend the line so as to keep the fly fishing at a controlled speed and well ahead of the main flyline. This is the key to successful fly presentation, in which the salmon in its lie is exposed to the sight of the fly moving at the speed and angle we want, without it seeing the heavy shadow or silhouette of the flyline. A successful mend involves compensating for the tendency of the line to belly away downstream by creating a reverse belly in the opposite direction, upstream and into the main flow of the current.

Mending the line is a matter of a succession of repeated actions, at least in the case of a fully floating line. A sinking or intermediate line, on the other hand, can usually only be mended once, and then only with accurate timing, just as the outstretched line kisses the surface of the water as the forward cast ends. Then it is just possible to twitch or flick the rod tip in such a way as to put one quick upstream curve in the line, before it sinks and is carried down and across the river by the pull of the current. But with a fully floating line it is possible – and necessary – to create a succession of these upstream bellies in the flyline, to offset the constant pulling of the current on the line and to keep the fly fishing at the desired speed and depth.

When correctly carried out, a mend will lift and reposition most or all of the flyline, while having little or no effect on the fly in the form of tugging or twitching. This may seem impossible, since line and leader and fly all are directly connected, but with practice it is readily done.

Like most aspects of casting and fly manipulation this is easier to understand in action or diagramatically, rather than in words. But imagine you are standing on the left bank of a river, or perhaps wading in the current a short distance out from the left bank. You have just cast out and across the river, almost at right angles to the direction of the stream. Your flyline, leader and fly land gently in a straight line out from the tip of the rod, and you have brought this to rest at the end of the cast, pointing upwards at about 40 degrees from the horizontal. Between the rod tip and the water the line hangs in a slack loop, and this element of slack line forms the beginning of your eventual mended loop or upstream belly. The action of mending the line begins with a smooth downstream movement of the rod tip, which has the effect of increasing the amount of slack line, and continues with a raising and backward movement of the rod tip, which swings upstream level with or just past your right shoulder, lifting most of the floating line off the water and replacing it again on the surface with the line now curving upwards into the stream, instead of bellying away downstream. If this is done smoothly and fluently, the repositioning of the flyline will have had little or no twitching effect on the steady downstream progress of the fly, and will serve to slow its movement. The tip of your rod will have moved so as to describe a flattened loop or oval, and come to rest back at about the same angle as when the mending action began.

Before long – within a few moments, in fact – a new downstream belly will begin to form, and another mend will be necessary, and perhaps three or four more mends will be required to keep the fly fishing steadily throughout the fishing-out of that cast, before the line, leader and fly finally come to rest on the dangle directly downstream of you, and a new cast is called for.

When learning to mend line in this way, it is usually much easier to begin by casting somewhat down-and-across the current, perhaps at an angle of about 45 degrees, and, as success and confidence increase, gradually to increase the angle of your initial cast, until eventually you are casting almost square across the river. With practice you will be able to lift and reposition almost all the extended length of the flyline, and thereby to create the upstream belly closer and closer to the end of the line. This not only keeps the fly fishing at the desired depth and speed, but also ensures that it is always travelling down the pool well ahead of the main flyline, which we do not wish the fish to see. If you watch an expert at work, especially if you have a vantage point well above him, perhaps from a high bank or from a bridge, you will see the mending action creating a loop that flows out from his rod-tip and comes to rest well out and above the fly, so that the direction of the line across and down the pool forms a somewhat L-shaped profile, with the angle of the L slightly curved and steadily increasing as the cast fishes its way down the pool. Fishing the fly on a floating line in this way achieves great coverage of the water, as the fly tracks steadily down and across the pool, and with a succession of casts effectively covers virtually the whole width of the pool on all but the very biggest and widest of British and Irish rivers.

Chapter 13 Hooking, Playing and Landing Your Salmon

The take of a salmon is usually a slower and more powerfully deliberate action on the fish's part than the swirling rise of a trout or the dashing snatch of an energetic seatrout. If your fly is fishing high in the water you may see the boil and swirl as the fish rises and turns to take the fly, a sight quickly followed by a steady pull on the line. If your fly is fishing deeper you may see no sign of the fish as it takes the fly, and the signal comes in the form of that distinctively long, powerful pull on the line that resolves itself into a solid yet vibrant resistance as the hook finds a hold – surely the most thrilling sensation in all game fishing!

A salmon that comes to the fly from its resting place in its lie usually takes the fly as it turns and heads back for its lie. This means that, if all goes well, the resistance of the line and the angle of the fish's turn will pull the fly back into the corner of the salmon's mouth, where the hook will find a secure anchor point in the angle of the fish's gristly jaws – the so-called scissors hold, which is usually the most secure and reliable hooking place. In an attempt to ensure such a good hook hold, many flyfishers follow the tradition of giving the fish some slack line, the theory being that this will allow the salmon time and space to turn back towards its lie before the resistance

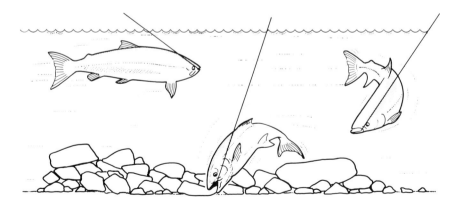

A salmon rising and taking the fly as it turns back and down again towards its lie, which often pulls the fly back into a secure hold in the jaws' 'scissors'.

of the line pulls the hook back into the scissors. Most anglers who follow this theory fish with a loop of slack line dangling between their forward rod hand and the reel, which they release when a salmon takes, thereby allowing the fish a few feet of slack before the tension of the line is applied.

This tactic will come as an unfamiliar practice to most trout fishers, who are accustomed to tighten into the fish immediately the take is felt, and, as with the loch dapping technique of waiting for a few moments before tightening on a fish, it calls for a good deal of self-control and restraint, since the natural impulse is to tighten into your fish just as soon as the take is felt.

In fact, there is a good deal of argument about exactly what is the best way to hook a salmon on the fly. Most traditionalists adhere to the principle of "throwing line to the fish", in the form of that loop of line, while a great many other highly successful anglers prefer to tighten as soon as they feel the pluck of the fish on the fly. The latter technique is sound and reliable, so long as it is linked to the holding of the rod at a relatively high angle as the fly is fishing. This high angle causes a concave loop of flyline to fall from the rod tip to the water, and the resistance of the fish's take is only felt when that portion of slack line has been taken up by the fish swimming off with the fly in its mouth. By that time, argue the tighten-at-once camp, the fish is already moving back towards its lie and the tightening of the line will have the desired effect of pulling the hook back and into a firm hold. If we consider the mechanics of this hooking theory, we can see that the loop of slack line below the tip of a high-angled rod is fundamental to its success. It is quite different from what happens when the rod is held at a low angle, which means that rod, line and fly are all more or less in a straight line, with little or no slack to allow the taking fish to move off before the tension

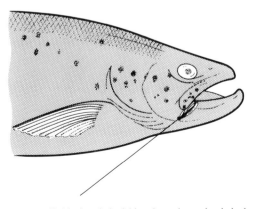

Scissors hook-hold. The most reliable hook-hold is when the point is lodged well past the barb in the gristly corner or scissors of the jaws' angle.

comes on the line. This is not recommended, since it is quite possible for the tight line to pluck the fly from the salmon's mouth before fish and line are at the best angle to achieve a sound hook hold.

A high rod angle is desirable from many points of view, and it keeps a good portion of the flyline out of the water and makes it much easier for the angler to mend his line, perhaps repeatedly, as the cast fishes down, all with minimal disturbance to the steady movement of the fly. If a salmon takes, the angler simply has to wait until that drooping loop is pulled upwards and the resistance of the fish is felt on the now-tight line before he tightens into his salmon. To give the fish yet more slack line at this stage is to delay unnecessarily the setting of the hook, and makes it more likely that the fish may spit out the fly before the hook has found a good grip. If it is necessary for any reason to fish with the rod held at a low angle – low overhanding branches are a commonly encountered example – then it is wise to release a few feet of slack line before you tighten on the fish, but if the rod angle is high that inevitable concave parabola of line below the rod tip should provide all the slack that is required.

Many trout fishermen are accustomed to playing their fish with their casting hand holding the rod and their free hand manipulating the line, recovering or releasing the line that is allowed to hang loose by his side. This is probably fine for trout of moderate size, but is unsuitable for playing a salmon. As soon as you have tightened into the fish and have achieved a steady tension on the fish, any loose line should be quickly wound back onto the reel, and the remainder of the battle carried out by playing the fish off the reel. Apart from the fact that this method avoids risky loops of line that can so easily tangle and snag, this is the only way in which you can employ the drag of the reel's mechanism as part of your playing of the fish. If the fish makes a run, it pulls out line against the check or drag of the reel's braking system, possibly modified by the further pressure of your cupped hand against the reel's exposed rim. This maintains a firm and even pressure on the fish, and it is only by sustained strain on the fish that we can wear down its powerful resources of strength and bring it beaten to the net. Use of the reel is almost always the best means of recovering line when the fish's movements make that possible, and likewise it is the best way of allowing the fish to take out line when it makes a dash or a run.

One of the few occasions when hand-lining is essential will occur if a fish suddenly makes a fast run back towards you, at a speed which is too great for the reel to recover line; and if this happens your only sure way of keeping the line taut and maintaining a strain on the fish is to strip the line in quickly by hand. But having done this, do not delay in winding the line you have recovered back onto the reel and resuming the normal procedure of playing the fish off the reel. Coils of slack line hanging down by your side are difficult to control, and may cause a snag or tangle that will lose you the fish.

Once you have tightened into your fish and it is firmly on, do not attempt to play it while wading deep. Instead, make your way carefully back to the bank, or at least into water no more than a foot or so deep, and then you will be able to concentrate fully on playing the fish, instead of trying to maintain a firm wading stance out in the water. Most importantly, once you are back in the shallows or on the bank, you are infinitely more mobile and can move readily to maintain an optimum position relative to the fish. It is sometimes possible to hook, play and land a salmon without moving your feet an inch, but it is asking for trouble to get yourself into a position from which you cannot move quickly and easily if the fish's fight makes it necessary to do so. The geography of the river and its banks will largely dictate what moves are possible for both fish and fisherman, but as a general rule you should aim to keep downstream of the fish at all times, if rocks and trees and other obstacles will allow you to do so. A downstream position gives you a much better measure of control over the fish in play, and subjects the salmon to the twin forces of the current and the tension of your rod and line.

Maintaining that tension is generally all-important, but there are times when it can be hazardous. For example, if the fish jumps, it is madness to

Unless wading conditions make it impossible, always get to the bank and play the fish from there.

allow it to fall back onto a tight line. If it does, the leader will probably snap, or the hook will pull out, and that is your fish gone. As soon as the fish jumps, smoothly dip your rod tip and allow the fish to splash back on a slack line, but take up the tension again quickly and smoothly the moment it is back in the water.

The tension of the line and the relentless spring of the rod will gradually wear down the fish's vitality, but a salmon can resist powerfully if that tension pulls against it more or less in line with the axis of its body and the direction in which it swims. Much more effective is tension that continually pulls the fish off balance, and this is traditionally known as "side-strain", simply because the strain is applied to pull the fish off balance to the side, and away from the direction in which it is trying to make its escape. Steadily repeated loss of swimming balance is a powerful factor in wearing down a salmon's resistance, and it is always most effectively achieved by watching the movement of the fish in play and maintaining your rod-and-line tension at an angle to the direction the fish is trying to take. This, like fishing the fly and hooking the taking fish, is always best achieved by maintaining a rather high rod angle, which helps keep line out of the water and allows you to make maximum use of the springy power and shock-absorbing qualities of your rod. Side-strain does not mean dropping your rod towards the horizontal and pulling against the fish with a sideways sweep of the rod,

Maintain a high rod point and keep tension on the fish, using the powerful spring of the rod to wear down its resistance.

although a good many photographs in books and magazines showing this curious rod position have been misleadingly captioned as revealing the angler "applying side-strain". The side involved is not your side, but a sideways angle relative to the direction in which the fish is trying to move. The aim is to disrupt the salmon's equilibrium in the water as an important part of wearing down its fighting energies.

Asking how long a salmon will fight before it is grassed is rather like asking how long is a piece of string. So much depends on the energy and size of the fish, the nature of the water in which it has been hooked, and the angler's skill in applying the wearying strain of rod-and-line tension. A general rule of thumb is sometimes quoted, indicating something like 10-12 minutes to play out a good 10-pound salmon, with perhaps another minute to be added per pound of the fish's body weight. Like most rules-of-thumb this is only a generalisation, and precise timing has no part in the adrenalin-pumping excitement of actually playing a fish. Like every moment of high human excitement, time means little, and, depending on your temperament, the whole affair from hooking to landing may seem either to have taken an age or else just slipped by in a blurred frenzy of activity. It is only the coolest and most experienced angler who will glance calmly at his wristwatch once the fish is firmly on and refer to it again when the fish is safely in the net.

The successful conclusion to the playing of the fish is the landing or beaching of the beaten salmon. It is important to be able to judge when a fish is thoroughly played out and ready to be netted, tailed or beached, and the surest sign is when the fish rolls over onto its side and presents its silvery flank upwards. This rolling off balance is the best indicator that the fish's energies and resistance are almost exhausted. Just because you have been able to coax a salmon right in close to you, and perhaps right under the bank you are standing on, is no guarantee that it is ready to be netted or tailed. So long as the fish maintains an upright balance it almost certainly still has reserves of energy to make a final dash for freedom, especially if it is suddenly frightened by your shadow or silhouette hovering darkly above it. Probably more well-hooked salmon are lost at or near the net than at any other stage in the fight, so a disciplined and orderly landing procedure is essential.

If you have a capable companion or a gillie to wield the net, it is often possible to grass your salmon rather more quickly than if you are fishing quite alone. On your own, it is always best to play the fish until its behaviour indicates that it is wholly exhausted and spent, at which point you can unhitch your net or tailer from its lanyard and manipulate this with one hand while the other keeps the rod point high and maintains a tight line on the fish. (Exceptions to this are when you can see that the fish is either a

Here one angler helps his friend by netting the fish. The beaten fish is drawn over the submerged net, never scooped out.

kelt or a gravid pre-spawner, in which cases you will wish to get the fish in and release it as quickly as possible, without playing it to exhaustion – and you may even adopt tactics that are designed to give such fish every chance of throwing the hook and escaping without any further ado.)

If you have a helper to handle the net or the tailer, make sure that he or she always keeps on the downstream side of you, and out of your way until an opportunity of netting the fish seems imminent. Then they should move in to your side, keeping a low profile so as not to get in the way of you or your rod and line, and so as not to alarm the fish by obvious bankside movement. If the fish is thoroughly played out and has tipped over onto its side in final submission, the net or tailer should be extended and held quite still while you, the angler, draw the fish in closer, over the submerged net or close to the tailer's noose. (On no account try to get the fish with a scooping or sweeping movement of the net or tailer.) Then a brisk yet smooth lift of the handle of the net or tailer should secure the fish – and well up the bank with him without delay, for the administration of the priest and then the removal of the hook. Plenty of fish have been lost by flapping out of the net and back into the water once the hook has been removed!

Now is the time to reel in, hook your tail fly into the keeper ring or fly-holder, and place the rod somewhere safe – and certainly never flat on the bank where it may be trodden on! – and take a good look at your prize. He

Drawing a beaten fish over the net.

deserves admiration and respect, this amazing migrant whose trans-oceanic wanderings have finally brought him back to the river of his birth. Is he fresh and silvery? Are there sea-lice in evidence? Or has he begun to colour up after re-entering freshwater a week or two earlier? Are there any marks on him, that might indicate a seal attack, or an encounter with a net? Is it a hen or a cock fish, and does it show any signs of coming into spawning condition? To inspect a newly caught fish like this is not only an exercise in well-deserved admiration and respect: it is also an opportunity to learn a little bit more about the species, and to compare this fish's style and con-formation with that of other salmon from other waters. A companionable dram is timely, too – what Victorian salmon fishers in Ireland used to term "the christening of the fish", in tribute to this success and with a toast in eager expectation of the next one.

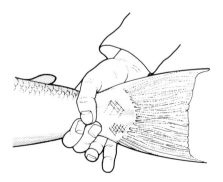

The correct hold when tailing a salmon by hand. The wrist above the tail forms a natural handhold, and the stiff outer rays of the tail prevent the fish from slipping out of the grasp.

Releasing a fish – here, a thin kelt. Steady it in the water, head into the current, until it regains its balance and orientation.

The prize: a specimen salmon. Take time to admire it, and look critically for signs of parasitic sea lice, net marks, damage by seals or otters, and other physical markings.

Chapter 14   Salmon in Stillwaters
– a neglected option

Salmon are the premier game fish of rivers, and we may tend to think of salmon fishing as an activity pursued exclusively by the side of running water, whether it is the trilling of a Highland spate stream, the impressive sweep of a big east coast river like Tweed or Tay, or the silent power of a southern chalk stream like the Frome or the Hampshire Avon. Ask most salmon flyfishers about their favourite waters, and you will find that they usually mention a stretch of flowing water.

But salmon also occur in stillwaters, especially those Scottish lochs and Irish loughs which are parts of river systems connecting with the sea, and to which upstream fish access is not barred by insuperable natural waterfalls or man-made dams and barriers. A loch of this kind can, after all, be viewed not just as a water-filled hole but as a massive widening and deepening of the river, one vast pool, in fact, in which the speed of the water flow is greatly reduced but not completely eliminated, before the waters converge at the outflow and the system once again assumes the character of a river on its course to the sea. Salmon running up such river systems to their eventual spawning grounds upstream of the lochs clearly must pass through them en route, and salmon will readily rest for some time in a loch, just as they will take up station in a lie in a river pool.

Loch fishing for salmon is too often neglected by salmon fishers in general and by flyfishers in particular. This is strange and unfortunate, and the potential of lochs for providing good salmon flyfishing should be more widely recognised. Fishing conditions and tactics on lochs are, not surprisingly, rather different from those we find on rivers. We exchange the comparative intimacy of a relatively narrow flowing stream for the broad acres – perhaps hundreds or even thousands of acres – of open loch waters. This is not to every salmon fisher's taste, and there is no denying the special fascination of fishing the lively flows and runs and pools of a river. But loch salmon represent a fresh challenge, and loch fishing has a charm all its own. It is a pity therefore that many dedicated and experienced salmon river fishers have never tried flyfishing on a loch. (It may also be noted that there a good many very keen and successful loch salmon experts, especially in Ireland and western Scotland, who are seldom if ever seen on the banks of a river, and they too are missing an important dimension of the sport.)

There are two main reasons why I have chosen to devote quite a large

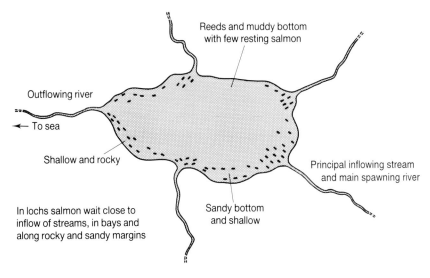

Reeds and muddy bottom
with few resting salmon

Outflowing river

← To sea

Shallow and rocky

Principal inflowing stream
and main spawning river

In lochs salmon wait close to
inflow of streams, in bays and
along rocky and sandy margins

Sandy bottom
and shallow

Salmon lies in a loch.

proportion of this book to loch fishing for salmon with the fly. First, this is a
dimension of salmon flyfishing which has been largely neglected by British
writers since the 1930s, and I believe it is an important aspect of salmon
fishing which deserves to be much more widely known and practiced. Many
salmon anglers who really ought to know better are largely unaware of the
potential of the flyrod on a loch, and labour under the misapprehension that
the only way to catch a salmon is by more or less by chance, while
mindlessly trolling a Devon minnow or a Toby behind a boat. (In fact,
trolling need not be mindless, and has its own skills and secrets.) Secondly,
and importantly for the newcomer and the flyfisher on a budget, salmon
lochs offer opportunities for good sport which is still readily available at
modest cost. What follows is an attempt to look in some detail at the ways
of salmon in lochs, and the best flyfishing tactics to adopt to catch them.

From a purely practical point of view, it is worth noting that some very
good catches of salmon can be made in lochs, and this tempting prospect is
made still more attractive by the fact that it is generally a great deal cheaper
than river salmon fishing of comparable quality. Two rods can often get a
day's salmon fishing on a loch, complete with a good boat and an outboard
engine, for about £25-£30, and sometimes for even less, when a single day
ticket for one rod on the river above or below that same loch may cost
several times as much. Many lochs are also readily fishable at short notice,
when you may have to wait for many years and then part with a very
sizeable cheque for the opportunity of a week's fishing on a coveted beat
somewhere on the river just a short distance above or below the loch. Loch
Brora in Sutherland is a good example of this. Even if you add the

additional cost of employing a boatman or gillie to take you out on a loch – about £25 per day at 1994 prices – you are generally still getting good salmon fishing at a very reasonable total cost.

The west Highlands of Scotland, the Inner and Outer Hebrides, Orkney and Shetland, and the west of Ireland all offer good salmon fishing on lochs, in addition to the trout and seatrout fishing for which they are perhaps chiefly known. One of the most consistently productive – and most exclusive – salmon fisheries in the world is the Grimersta system of lochs in the Outer Hebridean island of Lewis, a salmon flyfishers' Shangri La to dream about but, for most of us, never to be experienced. But readily accessible to the visiting flyfisher are the waters of Loughs Currane, Beltra and Melvin in Ireland, all of which are outstanding salmon fisheries, especially in the spring months, while very good sport is available in Scotland as far south as Loch Lomond and thence northwards and westwards in scores of lochs large and small, chiefly in summer and early autumn. The Irish lough salmon fisheries have been particularly well documented in Peter O'Reilly's excellent guide, *The Trout and Salmon*

High in the headwaters of the river system, this small loch has a good population of small salmon by late summer. Here I am preparing to set out, using a single-handed seatrout rod, with just enough ripple on the water to give animation to the two-fly cast.

Loughs of Ireland (1987, revised 1992), which provides copious information about access, where to obtain permits and tickets, hire of boats and locally successful fly patterns. Scotland's many salmon lochs deserve equally detailed treatment in an up to date guide, and Crawford Little's *Salmon and Seatrout Fisheries of Scotland* (1990) has already gone some way towards this.

Many salmon fisheries on river-and-loch systems are comparatively simple, consisting of one fairly sizeable loch with a single outflow to the sea. Loch Brora and the River Brora in Sutherland, and Loch Melvin and the River Drowes in Ireland are good examples of this type. Much more complex are systems such as the Grimersta in Lewis and the Delphi in Connemara, in which the ascending fish are confronted with a sucession of lochs, with connecting streams which offer a choice of directions in which the fish can run up. Yet within such intricate systems each fish unerringly manages to make all the right navigational turns to bring it back to the selfsame feeder stream in which it was hatched.

Loch and river systems tend for reasons of geography and geology to be more common in the north and west of Britain and Ireland, where glaciation has moulded the landscape, and where the lochs are accordingly often deeply gouged. Likewise the north-western rivers tend often to be spatey in type, drawing water down in a rush from steeply sloping land where there is a naturally fast run-off of rainwater. These areas tend also to get some of the highest rainfall anywhere in the British Isles. The natural tendency of floodwater to run quickly off steeply sloping ground has been further increased in recent times by extensive systems of arterial drainage on agricultural and afforested land. In places where formerly the blanket peat used to soak up a good deal of rainfall and release the water by steady seepage, today's conditions often mean that heavy rain is channelled quickly into a highly efficient system of gullies and drains, which greatly accelerate the rate of run-off and thus cause the streams and rivers to rise at great speed after heavy rain, and to discharge water at a much faster rate than in former times. On many such systems spates now tend to rise more rapidly, to run bigger, faster and dirtier, and to drop away much more quickly than they used to, and this can cause considerable problems not only for fisherman but also for the populations of fish, and this is discussed later in the chapter on conservation.

Rivers which discharge from large lochs in hill country are in general not nearly so spatey in character as those neighbouring streams which simply collect run-off water from the slopes of the land. While the headwaters of a hill stream can be quickly swelled by heavy rain, the large and deep body of water in a loch is not so readily affected by rainfall, however heavy or prolonged. The inflowing rivers may be rushing furiously and carrying down a large volume of coloured water and assorted debris, causing local discoloration where they enter the loch, but thereafter the loch acts like a large sump, slowing down and buffering the pell-mell rush of flood water. It also functions as a large and effective natural silt trap, into which the suspended particles of soil, peat and other detritus sink. This ensures that the outflowing water is generally little more than slightly coloured, even after continuous heavy rain. The outflow rate of water from a loch is mitigated to a large extent by the presence of that large body of water above it, which acts like a massive header tank by helping to maintain the flow in dry weather and also to buffer the effects of floodwater in periods of heavy rainfall. Although a free-draining river may rise and fall by perhaps as much as eight or ten feet between spates, a loch-fed river may not vary by more than a couple of feet between its maximum winter height and its summer low levels. The strength and direction of the wind can sometimes be as least as significant as the rainfall on loch-fed rivers. A typical west-flowing river-and-loch system may undergo an appreciable rise in river water levels when there is a strong easterly wind to push water downstream. This is not as dramatic as a flood but it is still important, and by the same token such a river may experience somewhat reduced water levels when there is a steady westerly wind blowing against the flow. In each case the effect of the wind is to bank up the loch water to leeward, i.e. downwind. This has the effect of pushing more water out and down the river when there is an offshore wind, and of partially stemming the flow when the water is backed up by an onshore wind.

Once in the lower river reaches of a loch-and-river system, salmon will move gradually upstream and eventually enter the loch, from which they will later move up still further into the smaller streams which feed the loch, where they will finally spawn. However, spawning does not take place until the late autumn and winter, and salmon may run into the river and loch many months earlier. In Ireland's Lough Gill and Lough Melvin, for example, salmon are known to run up into the loughs almost a full year before they spawn, ascending from the sea in late November and December and not spawning until the following October and November. The salmon that are the quarry in Loch Tay and Lough Currane when the first fishermen appear in February are not destined to spawn for at least another nine months. These and other fish which follow in the spring and summer have to wait for weeks and months before the arrival of autumn and the final onset of physical breeding condition, and, just as importantly, when the autumn rains have swollen the feeder streams sufficiently to allow the spawning fish to ascend into them from the waters of the loch. Many salmon therefore have an enforced period of waiting in lochs in spring and summer, just as early-run spring and summer fish linger in rivers, and it is during that waiting period that they are of particular interest to the salmon fisher.

On arriving at a salmon loch, probably the first question to spring to the mind of a visiting fisher is, "How on earth do I know where to begin to fish in such a large expanse of featureless water?" And for the flyfisher the second may be, "How do I fish a fly effectively for salmon in a loch when there is no current to give life to my fly?"

The answer to the first question lies partly in a general understanding of the typical ways of salmon, and partly in specific local knowledge built up over generations of fishing on the loch in question. As for the second problem of working the fly, the simple answer is to say that we move the fly and give animation to it in the water by making use of a different motive force – the strength and direction of the wind and the waves instead of the current of flowing water.

Salmon in freshwater are chiefly impelled by their singleminded spawning impulse, and that has implications for their behaviour and movements in lochs. Their "onwards and upwards" tendency makes them move up the river steadily as long as there is enough depth of well oxygenated water to allow them to do so. Once in the loch they will tend still to swim on, always influenced by the subtle and very much reduced currents which are still evident to their sensitive senses. However still the waters of a loch may appear to us, they are constantly flowing, albeit at a very much slower rate than the river flow, and the fish can detect this. The irresistible chemical invitation which calls them back from the sea is still carried to them in the gentle currents of the loch, and so they move ever onwards towards their eventual goal, those natal spawning streams. Salmon in a loch will therefore tend to congregate in the bays where the feeder streams flow in, and from which they will eventually ascend in the late autumn to spawn when their bodily condition and the water conditions permit. Other fish will move upstream behind them, following more or less defined routes through the loch, and stopping to rest periodically at various points en route, especially close to the shore and in the shallows around islands and underwater ridges, just as fish lie in holding pools in rivers before moving on further.

The bays and mouths of inflowing streams can be most attractive places for trout and salmon, and therefore happy hunting grounds for the flyfisher. Both species enjoy the freshness of well oxygenated water, especially if the weather is warm and other areas of the loch are becoming deoxygenated. Trout also enjoy the steady trickle of foods borne down on the current, while salmon are held by the constant attraction of the smells of the streams of their birth and youth.

The best conditions to encourage salmon to hold up in the bays of inflowing streams occur when the influx of water is steady and gentle. A heavy flow of water can draw salmon upstream into the headwaters too quickly for the loch fisher's liking, while dirty and debris-laden floodwater can drive the fish away from the bays in disgust and cause them to take up lies elsewhere in the loch, or to move about restlessly. Trout, in contrast, may be drawn in numbers to feed in the bays and on the fringes of the turbid water, attracted by the sudden influx of food items brought down by a spate. Sudden spates into lochs can also carry down a sudden flush of aluminium and other elements which salmon find harmful or distasteful, especially where stormwater runs off land which has been afforested with conifers.

Bearing this in mind, the loch fisher for salmon will probably be able to set to work with some chances of success, even on a totally unfamiliar loch and with no other hints or specialised local advice to help him, just as a salmon fisher who knows how to read the water might fare quite well among the pools and glides of a totally new salmon river. But when this general understanding of salmon and their ways in lochs is allied to detailed local knowledge or advice about a particular loch fishery, the chances of success are greatly increased.

Astute fishers on rivers try to read the water, using a combination of deduction, conjecture and educated guesswork to build up a mental picture of the underwater geography of a stretch of river, based on the flows they can see, the position of rocks and shallows, and other features. But skill in reading the water is no less a recipe for success when fishing a loch for salmon. There may be no obvious current and no midstream boulders to guide us, but we can deduce a great deal about a loch by simply studying the geography and geology of its setting. In doing this it is important to think of the loch not as a deep mass of water but as land under water, and thus to build up an impression of the underwater landscape. A lake set amid low pastures is unlikely to plunge to the depths which occur in a glaciated loch ringed by high peaks and steep slopes. Where the land gives way almost imperceptibly to the lake we can usually assume that the underwater profile continues at much the same angle, with the water becoming only gradually deeper. Where a steep heathery shore or a tumble of rocks dips into dark waters we can be equally sure that the submarine contours continue in a sharp drop into a considerable depth of water.

The accumulated wisdom of generations of salmon fishers, confirmed by modern technology, shows that salmon tend to lie in comparatively shallow water, and this is usually in the range 3-12 feet in depth. They will lie over loch bottoms which are rocky, gravelly or sandy, but generally avoid areas where there is weedy growth or where a muddy bottom is likely to be churned up and made turbid by the action of wind and waves. Salmon holding areas tend to occur along loch shorelines where a fairly gentle fringe of rocks or sand shelves gently into the water. They are also found where an underwater ridge of rocks, or a sand bar, or perhaps the drowned remains of a prehistoric lake dwelling or crannog creates a shallow zone in an otherwise open and deep part of the loch. Such favoured salmon lies also occur where a point or promontory sticks out from the shore, perhaps where a bay opens out into the main loch. These can all create what the Irish call good "salmon lodges", and every good boatman and gillie will know most of them on his home lochs. The visiting flyfisher, even if he has no source of local information, can still make some educated guesses, based on a critical look at a large scale map of the loch and its surroundings, and by a simple reconnaissance of the loch on his arrival.

Salmon in lochs often choose the sort of lies where you might expect to find a good specimen brown trout, lying individually or in twos and threes quite close to the shore and remaining in limited areas of comparatively shallow water. In this respect they behave differently from seatrout in lochs, which are more likely to be found in small shoals out over the deeper water and moving about a good deal. On many Scottish lochs and Irish loughs which receive runs of salmon and seatrout the local gillies may therefore choose to take their Rods to fish quite different areas, depending upon whether seatrout or salmon are the principal quarry. But that is not to say that the day's basket may not contain both salmon and seatrout, and perhaps some brown trout too. Such mixed baskets are especially character-istic of good summer days on the lochs of the Outer Hebrides and in the west and south-west of Ireland.

Modern technology comes to the assistance of the salmon flyfisher on lochs, supporting and extending generations of salmon fishers' observations by means of electronic depth sounders and fish-finders. This sounds very high-tech, especially for the newcomer to salmon fishing who is on a budget, and perhaps is even verging on the unsporting. But even a few hours afloat in a loch boat fitted with a fish-finder can be a great eye-opener, a fascinating insight into the underwater world so tantalisingly inaccessible to unassisted human senses.

Depth sounders and fish-finders do not only chart the underwater contours of a loch, confirming the presence of the deeps, the shallows and the ridges which earlier generations only guessed at. They can also reveal the presence of mid-water objects such as shoals of perch and charr, foraging trout – and salmon in their lies. Since the 1970s the miniaturisation and development of these sonar devices has made them accessible at a moderate price to fisheries managers and even individual anglers. Hummin'bird and Lowrance are two of the best-known names among manufacturers of compact fish-finders for portable use in small boats, and their products are now widely used in Britain and Ireland. A transducer mounted below the waterline emits and receives impulses which are displayed in numerical and graphic form on a compact screen on the main unit, and this can be readily placed on a thwart or a seat for easy viewing by an operator handling an outboard motor or at the oars. The Lowrance screen uses three fish-shaped LCD icons to depict fish in three size categories – small, medium and large – which correspond approximately to the relative sizes of a smolt or small trout; a catchable (i.e. about one pound) trout or charr; and a grilse or salmon (and perhaps also a specimen trout or pike).

The visual display can be accompanied by an optional audible alarm, which on the Lowrance model involves one bleep for a small fish, two bleeps for a medium sized fish and three quick bleeps for the largest category. This unmusical accompaniment can be useful to attract your attention, but may become maddening at other times. The bleeping becomes positively demented when the boat passes over a dense shoal of charr, for example, and a repeated triple-bleep noise may only serve to rub salt in the wound when you know you are drifting over well filled salmon lies but are unable to stir a fish to take your fly. At such times I have been very grateful for the option which allows me to turn that insistent audible tone off!

Whether seen on the LCD screen or indicated by bleeps, salmon positions can be plotted as you drift or motor slowly over a loch, and if this is done systematically throughout a whole season, or better still throughout a succession of seasons, it provides accurate data about salmon lies and movements. It not only indicates which sectors of a loch are best populated with salmon, but also shows the typical depths at which they tend to lie, and also if and how they respond to the daily cycle of sunlight and darkness, and to changing barometric pressure and variations in general weather conditions. All these factors may have a bearing on the tackle and tactics most likely to result in a tight line, a wet net and a salmon for the larder. In time this information builds up into an invaluable salmon map and diary, a sort of piscatorial almanac which can give sound guidance on the likely whereabouts of salmon in a loch at any particular time of the year. Such data are of enormous value to a fisheries manager, of course, and the salmon fisher who sets out on a loch with the benefit of this information is bound to have some advantage, even if it is only the confidence which so often brings success.

Before the newcomer undertakes loch fishing from a boat, it is as well to have a word about the boats themselves. There are two types of loch boat, in my experience. The good ones are a delight: the others are an abomination. A sound and well constructed loch boat which rides the water well, drifts steadily and is well fitted out internally is a pleasure to use, as enjoyable a mobile casting platform as you could desire for a long day's fishing. A boat like this is so obviously suited to its task that you tend to take it for granted. It behaves well, does everything you expect of it, and it gives you peace to get on with your fishing – and that, after all, is its *raison d'etre*. But everything changes when you find yourself stuck with a bad boat: suddenly it is all discomfort, frustration and very hard work, all of which distract from effective and enjoyable fishing. Remember the old soldiers' adage that "any damn fool can be uncomfortable", and give plenty of thought to planning your boat, engine, tackle, clothing and extra equipment so that nothing is forgotten and everything is conducive to comfort, safety and enjoyment.

A complete list of the undesirable qualities of a loch boat could fill many pages, but here are a few of the worst. First there is the matter of size. On an Irish or Hebridean loch of any size it will be uncomfortable and possibly even hazardous for two Rods to set out in a boat which is less than 14 feet in overall length. Tackle bags, a net, bags containing extra clothing, lunch etc. all take up space, and if your legroom is restricted, discomfort and cramp will ensue. A third person in the form of a gillie or a non-fishing friend in a small boat will make it decidedly crowded. A decent loch boat for any of the larger lochs should be in the range 16-19 feet long, and preferably at the larger end of this scale. My own Irish-made lough boat is 19 feet overall and is capable of taking two anglers (and, in my case, usually two dogs as well) and all their gear in total comfort for a long day in all but the roughest weather. One or two non-fishing passengers can also be fitted in, and when drifting in a moderate wind it is perfectly possible for a third Rod to fish by dapping from the central seat, while the other two fish by conventional wet fly methods in the bows and stern. Just try doing that in a 14-footer.

As to the boat's width, properly known as its beam, avoid boats of narrow construction. These tend to roll badly, which is particularly uncomfortable and tiring when you are drifting in a good breeze and a biggish wave. Every movement by any of the occupants, including casting, can make such a boat rock noticeably. It is tiring and eventually leads to soreness and stiffness in your back and stomach muscles if you have to spend the whole day compensating by continual adjustment of your balance in an unstable boat. This can be compared to the aching miseries suffered by a novice horseman after a long day in the saddle of a horse with an awkward action. A good loch boat will have a generous beam and remain steady when riding downwind on a drift. Gillies graphically describe such a boat as "taking a good grip of the water".

Since the 1960s fibreglass and injection-moulded plastic hulls have increasingly dominated the small boat market. This is a blessing in terms of boat maintenance, obviating the annual sanding down and painting rituals necessary with wooden boats. Synthetics are also largely corrosion free, and can be moulded to incorporate integral buoyancy chambers and other features which are useful for safety and general convenience. Fibreglass and plastic boats can also be handled and transported with a readiness which would be reckless with a wooden boat. A boat that has spent a full day out on a loch can be quickly hauled onto a trailer, lashed down and trundled home behind the family car, joggling unharmed over bumpy roads that would quickly shake a wooden hull to pieces.

However, many synthetic hulls are simply too light and buoyant to allow easy and enjoyable fishing. I have seen and had the misfortune to fish from a good many synthetic-hulled boats which ride far too high in the water, which catch the wind and therefore drift much too fast. Worst of all, many tend not to drift true and level, and have a tendency to swing round and drift at an angle, bow or stern foremost. Some swing to and fro alarmingly in a blustery wind or a choppy wave, and require continual attention to maintain an acceptable trim. This is tiresome for the boatman or gillie, and utterly exasperating for two Rods trying to cope without a gillie. Such a skittish and lively boat makes fishing a misery unless the Rods take turns on the oars, and this effectively halves the boat's total fishing effort. It is not, of course, impossible to find a synthetic hull which is pleasant to handle. The best of them are superb, combining the best qualities of wood and synthetics, handling easily and requiring minimal maintenance, but for each such paragon you are likely to encounter three or four which are unpleasant to occupy and handle.

Whether wooden or synthetic, a good loch boat should be correctly fitted out internally. That calls for thoughtful positioning of the thwart seats, otherwise a laden boat cannot be trimmed to ride and drift properly, and these should also be set high enough to allow the seated and casting angler to stretch his legs. Too low a seat invites discomfort and eventual cramp. A detachable high seat which can be laid transversely across the top of the gunwales is often useful, and this can be made quite readily from a suitable piece of planking with batons screwed onto the underside to help locate the seat and hold it in place.

A set of wooden or plastic hooks or slots on the inside of the boat or to the side of the thwarts will secure a number of rods when they are not in use, and greatly reduce the chances of rods slipping about and becoming entangled or even broken. A small locker beneath the bow seat can hold useful bits and pieces such as a spare set of rowlocks, and will keep cameras and other fragile items safe from wind and rain.

One of the greatest trials of any boat angler's patience is to endure a day's fishing in a boat fitted out with slotted-type detachable floor boards, especially if they are loose-fitting. A more damnable device could scarcely be devised. It will snag every loose coil of line; any flies or other small items you may put down or drop will roll under the slats and out of reach; and nets, basses, tackle bag straps and painter ropes will become caught up in them incessantly. Where a boat is fitted with detachable floor boards these should preferably be of absolutely flat plywood.

There should be two sets of rowlock sockets or thole pins, respectively fore and aft of the centre point of the boat's length. This will allow an oarsman a choice of two thwart seats, or alternatively two oarsmen can take an oar each to pull home into a stiff wind, in the event of the engine failing to start or running out of fuel, which are not unknown events on the lochs. The transom should be reinforced with a plate of stainless steel or zinc to allow an outboard engine to be clamped securely, and without the clamps digging into the wood of the transom boards. There should be a soundly anchored ring or loop of brass or stainless steel to which an outboard engine's safety rope can be tied with a proper quick release knot such as the tried and tested falconer's knot. No-one wants to see their valuable outboard knocked off the stern and lost in deep water, and a properly secured safety rope will prevent such a loss, which at the least will be expensive and may also be dangerous in poor weather on a big loch.

Finally, some sort of bailer should be carried. All wooden boats take in some water, and even synthetic hulls collect water in the form of spray or rain. A small plastic bucket is as good as anything, and a safety cord will prevent its loss overboard. Best of all is to fit a small bilge pump, activated by a single-handed lever and operated by the person occupying the stern seat.

Safety considerations when fishing from a boat are largely a matter of common sense, and yet it is amazing how often the most basic do's and don'ts are overlooked, either because the individuals involved are not habitual boat fishers, or because they become so absorbed and excited by their fishing that they do something silly. For example, every schoolboy knows you shouldn't stand up in a boat, and yet it is commonplace to see flyfishers repeatedly casting from a standing position in boats on every stillwater fishery around the country. To stand up in a small boat is instantly to magnify that boat's inherent instability. The much higher centre of gravity and the wobbliness of the average angler make it highly likely that he will stumble or lose his balance, and an awkward fall into the boat is the least that can happen. Much worse is if the stumbling occupant falls on top of one or two valuable carbon rods, shattering several hundred pounds' worth of tackle. Worst of all, and downright dangerous, is to risk a tumble into the water, perhaps knocking in one or more other occupants of the boat, and even causing a capsize.

Many trout anglers argue that they find it easier and less cramping to cast from a standing position. But cramp can be easily avoided by the sensible use of waterproof seat cushions and stretching your legs out while seated.

And the much higher profile of a standing angler makes him much more conspicuous to any fish nearby, which are therefore unlikely to be in a confiding taking mood. The standing flyfisher may be able to do a lot of casting but he is unlikely to catch many more fish.

Just occasionally a flyfisher simply has to stand up, or at any rate rise slightly from his seat, in order to cast out a longish line quickly to cover an individual feeding fish. This is more likely to be the case for the trout or seatrout angler than for the salmon flyfisher, and on the infrequent occasions when it has to be done the angler should move smoothly and carefully, and sit down again without delay. Standing up should be avoided altogether when conditions are at all rough, in a choppy wave or a surging swell.

If for any reason you simply have to move about in a boat, perhaps to change places at the oars or on the outboard controls, keep low in a crouching posture and move only one person at a time. But what if you do take a tumble or, for whatever reason, find yourself in the water? An angler who reckons himself to be a capable swimmer when taking a voluntary dip in a pool or on a beach, clad only in trunks and entering warmish water, may suddenly find he is a rather incapable swimmer when he is involuntarily immersed in cold water, and clad in several restrictive layers of fishing clothing. A buoyancy aid of some sort is highly advisable, and these are available in several forms.

The Heron company make excellent buoyancy waistcoats, which incorporate pads of non-absorbent foam and provide useful supplementary support to a person in the water. They also provide a useful extra thermal layer when you go fishing in cold weather. Orvis and Leeda distribute the Sospenders buoyancy braces, and Sospenders also make a handy Shorty Safety Waistcoat, and both can either be inflated orally before setting out, or by a CO_2 cylinder activated when a rip-cord is pulled. Other models are also available which have a water sensor built in, and these will inflate automatically when the wearer is suddenly immersed in water. (However, I understand these have sometimes been known to inflate unnecessarily and without warning when heavy rain or spray has activated the sensor, which must be a little alarming for the wearer!) These aids give about 15-18 pounds of buoyancy, which is better than it seems at first glance, and gives useful help to a person who is capable of swimming or treading water, and who is conscious. The makers do not claim that they will save a panicking non-swimmer, or someone who is unconscious and perhaps floating face downwards. For these a different design and a much greater degree of buoyancy are required, more akin to the full Mae West-style of life jacket, which supports the wearer's head well clear of the water and will automatically right an unconscious wearer who might otherwise be face downwards in the water. These are available from various makers, and can be obtained from any good boating equipment supplier or ships' chandlers. The best are not cheap, at around £150, but what price a life?

The handling of a fishing boat on lochs is an art best learned in the company of an experienced companion, and the newcomer to loch fishing should beware of setting out alone in anything but settled weather, especially with an unfamiliar boat and engine. Each boat and every outboard motor has its individual characteristics, and it is best to learn these well before you have to take action in a crisis. On Scottish lochs and Irish loughs a squall can sweep in without warning out of the blue of a good day, and then is not the time to discover that you are drifting fast towards a rocky lee shore and cannot get the knack of starting that temperamental engine. More curses and execrations have been expended on outboard engines than on any other mechanical device known to man.

Even if you are experienced in the handing of small boats on relatively sheltered stillwaters such as the reservoirs of the English midlands, do not underestimate the roughness of the conditions you may encounter on a western loch. On sizeable waters like Maree and Hope, Corrib and Conn, there can be sizeable waves and even a heavy swell running when a strong Atlantic wind blows up. In very rough weather fishing is best abandoned, and then it safest either to press directly upwind into the waves and swell, or to run before the weather and motor straight downwind. In either case take it steadily, and watch the conditions like a hawk. An unexpectedly heavy wave may hit the boat, and a following surge can sweep in over the stern and swamp the boat, if your engine speed is not carefully judged. Take the utmost care when motoring across the weather; there is the risk of broaching and capsizing if a big surge takes you beam-on. Above all, obey your instincts. Roughish weather can sometimes be good fishing weather, but only if you are still reasonably comfortable and confident. If rough weather fishing ceases to be a pleasure and begins to worry you, pull the starter rope and head for home and a hot bath. There will always be another chance tomorrow.

Chapter 15   Stillwater Tackle and Tactics

My choice of tackle for salmon flyfishing on a loch will be dictated by several factors. First, if I know that large spring fish are present, that the weather may be stormy and the water rough, and that the fish are tending to lie deep in cold water, I will opt for a 12-foot or 12½-foot rod, the longer and more powerful of my usual two loch rods for salmon. Here, if I wish to have a two-handed rod which is still just about light enough to be used for short spells as a single-hander, my choice is the Bruce & Walker Fish Eagle 12-footer, rated for a #8-10 line or their Hexagraph Hugh Falkus 12′4″ Grilse model, rated for a #10 line. For smaller summer salmon and grilse, with perhaps an occasional seatrout, in the warmer conditions from late spring onwards, I will usually favour my 10-foot or 10½-foot single-handed rods, which are quite powerful enough for even a biggish salmon, but are primarily intended for lighter use with a floating line. The 10-foot Bruce & Walker Fish Eagle rod, rated for a #7-9 line, is ideal, as is the more expensive B&W Merlin 10½-foot Stillwater model, rated for #6-8.

Nothing longer than 12½-foot is likely to be necessary for loch salmon, except perhaps when dapping is the chosen technique, and more of that later. Nor will I readily use a rod shorter than 10-foot when fishing from a boat, since anything less is unlikely to give me the control over the line and flies to enable me to work them to best advantage. The successful tripping of a bob-fly, especially close to the boat and in those critical moments just before the lift-off for another cast, is infinitely easier to achieve with a longish rod. In addition, a shorter rod does not give such good control when playing a salmon, especially if it should make a powerful run close to the boat, or, worst of all, under it. It is perfectly possible to hook, play and net a sizeable loch salmon with a 8½-foot or 9-foot trout rod, and many a trout fisher has had that pleasureable challenge when a salmon has unexpectedly taken one of his cast of trout flies. But when salmon are the primary quarry a rod of more appropriate length and power is advisable.

But avoid going to the other extreme. You may readily use your 15-footer when fishing a fly for salmon from a boat on a big powerful river like Tweed or Tay. Then, having hooked your fish, your boatman will get you quickly to the bank and you will conduct the fight and conclude the matter from there, with your feet on the ground and the fish enjoying all the benefits of a strong river current to assist its battle. On a sizeable river a long rod helps to dominate a fish in play, but anyone who undertakes a day's loch fishing with a big-river salmon rod is likely to exhaust himself unnecessarily by wielding an excessively long and heavy rod. The pleasure of flyfishing from a boat soon evaporates when tiredness sets in, and no-one can fish effectively when he feels weary and his concentration flags.

It is rarely necessary to cast a long line when fishing from a boat on a loch. The 30-yard and longer casts which can be so necessary and productive when fishing a biggish river have really no place in loch fishing, so the casting power of the rod-and-line combination need not be more than moderate. Much of the time the loch fisher will cast no more than 12-15 yards, and often he may barely use more than a couple of rod-lengths of line, especially when drifting over shallow lies and close to the loch shore. I therefore prefer to use a line rated for the upper weight indicated for the rod, so as to load it more effectively when fishing a short line. My Fish Eagle 12-footer, rated for lines in the range #8-10, will therefore normally be used with a #10 line. This will fish well on the usual downwind drifts and when casting across the breeze, and will also allow me to push a shortish line effectively into a strong wind if it should occasionally be necessary.

The general shortness of line used in loch flyfishing means that the regular loch fisher can lighten his rod-reel combination and fine-tune his tackle by cutting down his fly lines from the usual 30 yards to perhaps 20 yards or even less. This reduces the total bulk of the line on the reel, and enables a rather smaller, and therefore lighter, reel to be used. Backing line is of course much finer and less bulky than the main fly line, and the loch fisher needs to ensure that he has enough of this on his reels. I would be

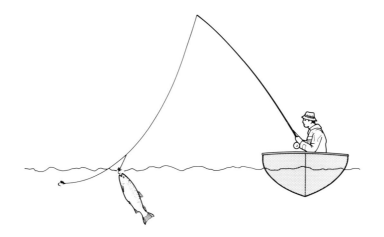

Fishing shortish lines while drifting beam-on to the wind. The speed of the boat's drift and the depth at which the flies are fished should be adjusted to suit the water temperature.

unhappy about having less than 150 yards of approximately 25lb backing, needle- or nail-knotted to my 20-yard or longer fly line. Despite the comparative freedom of a loch's open waters, salmon in stillwaters tend not to make the very long runs which are common among salmon in large pools on big rivers, but 150 yards of backing still provides a sensible insurance against the day when a big loch fish takes the fly and then attempts to dash all the way back to Greenland.

The typical Scots and Irish technique for salmon flyfishing from a loch boat is not radically different from that which is so generally successful for seatrout and brown trout. A shortish floating line is cast downwind from a boat drifting beam-on to the breeze, and the fly or team of flies is fished in the upper few feet or inches of the water. Often this is quite adequate in late spring and summer, when the higher water temperatures have made salmon less sluggish than in the early months of the season, and thus more ready to leave their lies and surge upwards to take a fly which it has seen in mid-water or close to the surface.

When I am fishing favourite drifts over known salmon lies on familiar lochs from May onwards I will usually cast a line of not more than about

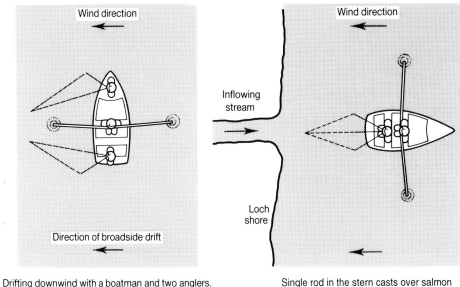

Drifting downwind with a boatman and two anglers.

Single rod in the stern casts over salmon lies where river flows in, while boatman holds boat in position with oars.

1.   Drifting downwind with a boatman and two anglers.

2.   Drifting over salmon lies at the mouth of an inflowing river. The gillie (or an electric outboard) holds the boat stern-on to the shore and brings the angler systematically over the lies.

12-15 yards, allowing it to flow out ahead of the drifting boat and giving it a moment to settle before I begin to raise the rod point and establish the close contact with the flies which allows me to control the pace and direction in which I retrieve them. Typically, my leader will be about 10-12 feet long and ungreased so that it sinks readily with the fly or flies. A two-fly cast, one on the point and the second on a dropper, will usually fish in the top 18-36 inches of the water, and if I choose a bushy and buoyant pattern for the dropper it may float and dibble along the surface at all times, while the point fly probably fishes at no more than 9-12 inches.

For deeper fly presentation I will turn to a medium- to fast-sinking line, perhaps teamed with a single larger or heavier fly, or a cast of two flies with a large and heavy, or smaller and leaded, pattern on the point and a lighter pattern on the dropper.

In really cold water conditions when the fish are lying deep and are moving slowly, the flies and their presentation should be judged accordingly, and then I may resort to a combination of line and flies which sink fast and fish deep. A fast-sinking line, and even an ultra-fast sinker as a shooting head, can play a useful role when fish lie deep and take slowly, and the best conditions are when there is only a light breeze. Then the boat drifts slowly, a longish line can be cast well ahead of the boat, and allowed time to sink before a slow retrieve begins. The object here, as in spring fishing in cold conditions on a river, is to present a fly deep in the water and moving slowly and close to the fish, allowing any salmon lying there to have a good close view of the fly before (we hope) they move a shortish distance to take it.

Unfortunately the coldest water conditions on lochs in February and March seldom coincide with gentle winds. A stiff breeze and a choppy wave are more likely, and then a free-drifting boat may move too quickly to allow time for the line to sink adequately. Instead it will tend to drift down on the line, the flyfisher will lose direct contact with the fly, and the line and leader may even wind up (literally!) under the keel and entangled with the boat. The obvious method of slowing the rate of drift is by hanging a drogue over the upwind beam of the boat, or in one of the other positions which can put the boat on an angled or bow-first drift, according to what is wanted. The best system for allowing a drogue to be altered so as to change the angle of the boat's progress is to have a fixed line running from bow to stern, with the drogue rope tied to this at right angles with a running knot such as a clove hitch. The sliding knot can then be pushed up or down the rope to alter the attitude of the boat's drift. A drogue can help to establish a considerably slower rate of drift than would otherwise be possible, and this allows time for the fly line and leader to sink sufficiently ahead of the boat, and a deeply sunk fly can then be fished slowly and presented more effectively close to the fish.

It is worth mentioning, however, that your wonderfully effective drogue can suddenly turn into a disastrous trap for the unwary angler if you should let your line – or worse, a line with a salmon attached to it – get tangled in it. As soon as a fish is on, your boatman or your fishing partner should immediately get the drogue out of the water and into the boat, stowed well out of the way to avoid mishaps. He should also have the presence of mind to realise that there is no point in rowing or starting up the engine while the drogue is still in the water. A horribly tangled propeller or even a capsized boat may be the result. And if you should happen to be fishing alone, try at all costs to keep the fish in play on the downwind or crosswind sides of the boat. (Note that this differs from the usual practice when fishing from a free-drifting boat, when it always makes sense to get your fish round and play it on the windward beam, with the boat tending to drift safely away from the fish and the line). A salmon which runs under the keel or around the upwind side will almost certainly snag your line on the drogue, and a sad parting of the ways is then almost inevitable. I know of one single-handed flyfisher who realised that a powerful fish was about to run upwind, whipped out a sheath-knife and cut his drogue adrift, and still lost the fish as the line sliced round and snagged in the abandoned and slowly sinking drogue.

The deeply sunk line is a proven but still little used method of taking early spring loch salmon on fly in cold water conditions, when most salmon fishers will spend the day trolling with oars or, more likely, with an outboard engine ticking over at minimum revs. A silver springer taken on the fly is an especially sweet reward for your efforts, and brings well deserved accolades when the boats return at dusk to the jetty and it turns out that all the other fish have been taken on deep trolled yellow-belly Devons. This method with the deeply fished fly deserve to be more widely known and more regularly used.

The traditional tactical approach to loch fishing with fly tackle for salmon is not much different from loch trouting. The essential ingredients are a comfortable loch boat drifting beam on down the wind, with one or two anglers casting a shortish floating line "over the front" and downwind, using a leader with two flies, one on the point and the other on a dropper. Countless thousands of salmon have fallen to just such tactics, and it remains an excellent method of fishing for loch salmon from late spring onwards.

My general rule of thumb is to use a leader of slightly greater length than my rod. Here I use the term leader to include not only the length of nylon to which my flies are tied, but also the 18-inch butt of heavy (about 25-30lb b.s.) monofilament which is needle-knotted to the end of the flyline. Thus when I have rigged up my 10½-foot single-handed loch rod ready to set out,

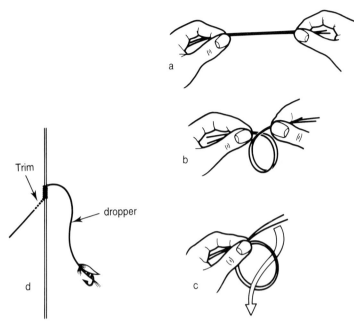

Line, butt and leader, with dropper.

the end of the flyline will just protrude a few inches outside the tip ring of the rod, the monofilament butt will reach a further 18 inches or so down the rod, followed by the lighter line of the cast. This extends down the rod, is looped round the reel seat, and the tail fly is led back by the rod and hooked into the butt ring or the one above it, which thus acts temporarily as a keeper ring. My 12-foot and 12½-foot loch rods will usually be similarly rigged, with an overall leader length not less than the rod length. Only in calm, low water of great clarity is it sometimes necessary to use a longer leader, to keep the potentially fish-frightening line well away from the fly, and when fishing a deeply sunk fly in cold water early in the season a total leader length (butt plus cast) of only 6 or 7 feet may be quite sufficient.

Let us suppose that it is a mild June day of intermittent cloud and sunshine, with a pleasant warm breeze blowing and stirring up a good fishing wave on the loch. In such classic loch flyfishing conditions I will use leader line of 10lb b.s., and will be reassured by the knowledge that the wave will help to conceal the leader line from the fish. But when fishing a large and heavy fly deep in the water under the leaden skies of February or March, with a typical rolling surge on the loch, I will readily go up to 14-16lb b.s. nylon on a short (6-8 foot) leader. Alternatively, if the water is warm, low and calm in summer I will drop down to as low as a 6lb line and use a longer leader. Many a summer salmon and grilse has been hooked and netted by a loch fisher out after trout and using nothing more than a 4lb leader, but such light line can never be recommended specifically for salmon fishing. The risks of a break and the loss of a fish with a fly in its mouth are simply too great.

If I am fishing in traditional loch fashion, I will usually have a two-fly combination, and this involves having a dropper on the leader. It is possible to buy readymade nylon leaders with single, double and even triple droppers, and although these are handy for the trout flyfisher I prefer to make up my own for salmon. Not only is it cheaper, which appeals to my sense of thrift; it also gives me the flexibility to vary my leader lengths and the relative position of the dropper. For a loch leader for use on this near-perfect June day we have imagined, I will use either a length of 10lb nylon or two lengths of differing strengths, one of 10lb for the upper cast and the dropper, tapering down to 8lb for the lower part of the cast and the point fly. In bright conditions I may even incorporate a third weight of nylon, to give a final 3-4 foot length of 6-7lb line at the point. This tapered profile gives a good turn-over when it is cast, and is probably best when you intend to fish with the smaller of your two flies on the point. But if I use 10lb nylon throughout I will not be at any practical disadvantage in fly presentation if I use flies of equal sizes, or even opt to put the larger fly on the point.

Most flyfishers have their own preferences for the distance between the tail fly and the dropper. In fact it is worth keeping an open mind about this, because flexibility can pay off in terms of fish caught. Sometimes you may wish to have your tail fly fishing relatively high in the water while your dropper fly bobs along on or just breaking the surface, which calls for a short distance between dropper and point, perhaps no more than 3-4 feet. At other times you may want to have a larger or heavier tail fly fishing deeper in the water, and then a dropper-to-point distance of 7-8 feet may be indicated. It is easy to spend a few minutes making up a selection of casts of varying specifications, and when fishing you can keep them to hand in individual clear plastic envelopes or on cast holders in your tackle bag or in a vest pocket – clearly marked, of course, so that you know what is what.

A floating line may seem to be the obvious choice for short casting and fishing a two-fly team from a boat, but it confers little advantage and may often be a definite disadvantage. Because it is intended to be buoyant, a floating flyline of any weight is sure to have a greater bulk and a bigger diameter than a sinking or intermediate line of the same line weight rating. Bulky line offers more wind resistance than thin line, it is more easily caught by the breeze, and the tugs and tweaks imparted by the wind to the line and thus to the flies can be excessive in a strong wind. On a blustery day the line and the flies can be whipped about very quickly, and the angler does not have total control over the behaviour of his flies.

When flyfishing from a drifting boat the longish rod and relatively short length of line cast should mean that the angler is in close command of his flies at all times. A longish rod held at the high angles which are usual in boat fishing keeps a lot of the flyline clear of the water, and ensures that the rest does not sink too deeply. If the line is of a sinking or intermediate type it does not offer too much resistance to the wind or to the surface movement of the waves, so that unwanted random movement of the flies is greatly reduced. A sinking or intermediate line cuts clearly into the water and sinks well down or hovers just below the surface, where it is out of the wind and the worst of the surface disturbance. An intermediate or slow sinking line is also a bonus on very calm days, reducing the surface disturbance caused by a floating line and helping to keep the flyline as unobtrusive as possible to the fish.

Furthermore, sinking and intermediate lines tend to be made in more sombre colours than floating lines, and experience leads me to believe this is significant in terms of fishing success. There is no denying the visibility of a floating line coloured white, pale iced-blue or light eau-de-nil, but when these are combined with the shiny surface of modern plasticised lines we have a recipe for a line which can flash brightly when it is cast, especially when it is flicked to and fro in a series of false casts. This seems almost guaranteed to alarm any fish, and should be avoided for that reason. A light coloured line floating on the surface is also liable to pick up and reflect sunlight, and to give the impression of a firmer and harder silhouette than that of a dark coloured floater. However, it has been maintained that a pure white sinking or intermediate line is actually less conspicuous to fish when it is under water than, for example, a dark brown or grey line. Light colour in a floating line therefore seems to be a liability, at least when boat fishing, although they may have a useful role to play in other styles of fishing, especially for nymph and dry-fly fishing on rivers and when night fishing for for seatrout. But when salmon fishing on lochs, it's best to leave your bright white floaters at home.

The choice of a suitable reel for loch fishing is not a difficult one. The reel's function is, as always, to store line and backing when it is not required, and to regulate the running-off of line when a fish is hooked and being played off the reel. There is no need for the massive line capacity we need when fishing a really large river with a long rod and a heavy line, so the wide-drummed 4½-inch diameter reel which will take a #12 floating line and 200+ yards of backing is simply too big. A normal length of #8-10 line and 150 yards of 25-30lb backing is readily accommodated on something rather smaller and lighter, and if you choose to fine-tune your loch lines by cutting them down to about 18-20 yards, a further saving in bulk line capacity is possible.

All good modern fly reels should have a smooth drag, whether this is in the form of a disc brake or the more usual ratchet and pawl system, and allied to this should be an exposed drum rim, for hand pressure to be applied when a fish is in play. The best reel engineering tends always to be expensive, and my first choices would be from Hardy, Leeda's System Two and Orvis; but among the lower priced reels I have had good service from Shakespeare Beaulite and Condex models, in both 3½-inch and 4¼-inch diameters. The latter size, with a normal width spool, is perhaps the best choice for loch fishing.

The downwind drift with one or two rods fishing over the front is so commonly seen on Scottish lochs and Irish loughs that you might almost be forgiven for imagining that no other loch flyfishing methods are available. In fact, there is some variety in the effective presentation of a fly to salmon from a boat.

A straightforward downwind drift is fine if the wind is in just the right quarter to enable you to cover the water you want to. But the angle of the breeze need be no more than a point or two off that ideal bearing for you to find that your chosen water is simply not fishable in a simple unregulated drift. That is when the effects of the wind on a bobbing boat need to be modified by other motive power. Traditionally this is supplied by the oars, and a good boatman will use them with steady and gentle skill so as to keep his boat on a good course which is the outcome of wind power from one direction and rowing effort in another. Today it is possible to replace the boatman's efforts with the power of a small electric outboard motor, and the practical effect on the boat's movement will be the same. In this way we can cope with a wind which deviates in direction by as much as 90 degrees from the desired line of drift. If the wind direction is more than 90 degrees off what you would like, you simply fish the water in the reverse direction, using oars or electric motor in the same way to counteract the natural angle of drift.

A most useful addition to any loch boat, and one that is increasingly seen these days, is a small auxiliary electric outboard motor. The larger petrol engined motor, usually in the range 3-6 horse power, does all the main work of getting the boat about the loch, onto the chosen drifts, and back to the jetty at the day's end, but the little electric engine can be brought into play while you are fishing a drift. Its gentle and silent power can be used to trim the direction and speed of your drift with great accuracy, enabling you to cover the water with optimum efficiency. Just a few seconds running can tweak the boat back onto the best line of drift, and this is achieved without any noise and with very little vibration.

A gently running electric outboard can also be used to hold the boat on station close to a known lie while you fish it thoroughly, just as a good boatman can hold you by careful use of the oars. But the electric engine may be even better for this purpose, with only a small propeller twirling silently instead of two oars dipping in and out of the water and casting two more silhouettes over any fish lying below.

The electric outboard also comes into its own in very calm conditions, when you may wish to inch the boat very slowly into position close to a lie, or perhaps to stalk an individual fish which you have seen. Trout fishers know the little electric motor's value in stalking and casting to individual rising fish, and the salmon fisher can also benefit from its careful use. It is usually best mounted either on the boat's transom well to one side of the petrol engine, or on the gunwale as close as possible to the stern, so that it can be operated easily by the person sitting on the stern seat.

Excellent electric outboards are available from Sigma and also from the American manufacturer MinnKota. A heavy duty 12-volt well cell battery is required, and I use one which is intended for Land-Rovers and tractors. It will often hold sufficient charge for two or three successive days' use, but if possible it should be topped up by means of a normal trickle-charger after each day's outing. One final use for an electric outboard which should not be overlooked is as a means of getting you home if you are well down the loch and the petrol motor simply won't start – not an unknown event with outboards. A low-powered electric motor won't rush you back at speed into a heavy swell and a stiff wind, of course, but it beats a long row any time.

Dapping is a flyfishing method which no stillwater gamefisher should neglect, whether his quarry be trout, seatrout or salmon. It has accounted for a vast number of fish, especially in summer and early autumn when water temperatures rise and the fish are inclined to be alert and willing to move quickly to take an attractive fly. Sadly, the art of dapping seems to have become devalued as a flyfishing skill, and is too readily dismissed as a simple and trifling affair, damned as "a method for old women". This is a pity, and very unfair, because while almost anyone can quickly be taught the basics of simple dapping, it calls for much more effort, concentration and thought if the fisher is to dap with full skill and effectiveness. After only 5-10 minutes a complete beginner can be dapping moderately well, as regards the simple holding of a rod so as to keep a buoyant fly bobbing and tripping over the waves, waves which in their turn are caused by that same wind which is essential for dapping with a blue-line. Mastery takes a little longer to achieve.

The essence of dapping is to deploy a combination of rod, line and leader so as to make use of the force of the wind to carry out line, leader and fly (or flies) downwind of the boat, and then to impart animated movement to the fly. The springy power of the rod is not required to project and present the fly, and for good fly presentation a long bar of solid wood or even iron would do almost as well when you are dapping. (But most definitely not, I hasten to add, once a fish is hooked and being played.)

When handled correctly, usually from a drifting boat, a dapping rig involves the fisher sitting with his back to the wind and holding his rod fairly upright most of the time. The wind catches the dapping line and carries it out downwind in an arching convex parabola, rather like the billowing spinnaker of a yacht. At the end of the dapping line comes a shortish (3-5 foot) length of nylon monofilament leader with a rather large, bushy and buoyant fly, occasionally placed on a dropper and partnered by a smaller and heavier "anchor" fly on the point. The latter is especially useful in rough water and a strong wind, when the elements combine to flick and swirl the blowline about in a haphazard and sometimes frenzied way. A small (size 10-12) fly, perhaps dressed on a "wee double" hook, is suitable on the tail, and this can be further dressed with a wrapping of lead wire or foil if additional weight is needed. A single lead shot may also be pinched onto the leader a few inches above the tail fly as a convenient means of adding additional weight if required.

For dapping on lochs it is possible – indeed advisable – to dispense with conventional flylines altogether. No line weight is required to load the spring of the rod for casting, nor will it be of any help. The wind is the critical motive force in dapping, and although there are occasions when a conventional flyline, especially a bulky floating line, is light enough to catch the wind and carry leader and fly off downwind, it lacks the gossamer lightness and high wind resistance which are the essence of the true, purpose-made dapping line. Originally of unbraided silk, modern dapping line, or floss, is composed of whispy synthetic threads which combine extreme lightness with a large surface area designed to present a large degree of resistance to the breeze.

Some guides to dapping suggest that a length of 30 or even 50 yards of dapping floss – i.e. a whole spool – should be attached to a conventional flyline, which in turn has a quantity of backing behind it. This is both unnecessary and expensive, and betrays a basic lack of understanding of how dapping works. No-one needs 30 yards, or even 30 feet, of blow-line. The best arrangement involves a length of 10-15 feet of dapping floss firmly and smoothly joined to a well-filled reel of heavy monofilament line. An oval sectioned line of 20-30lb breaking strain is best, similar to the kind of shooting line used in conjunction with a shooting head setup for river fishing for salmon. Oval or even flat monofilament is less subject to chronic twists or "line memory" than round-sectioned line, and is generally easier to handle.

The dapping floss, which nowadays comprises gossamer-light strands of nylon or similar synthetic, should be knotted at intervals of about 2-3 feet with a single overhand knot, to prevent the tiny individual strands from becoming separated and then tangled with the fly or the line. This can be a nightmare, especially if the floss has become wet. The floss-to-line join can be made with a smooth plastic patent connector, or with a whipping joint, and a smear of superglue over the finished join will make it slick and smooth. To the far end of the dapping floss is attached the dapping leader, which need be no more than 3-4 feet long, and for loch salmon I prefer a length of 10-12lb monofilament.

Purpose-made dapping rods are available, including telescopic fibreglass rods which fold down to around 30 inches and extend to total lengths of between 15 and 18 feet. Three-piece carbon fibre dapping rods are also made, including an attractively finished model by Grey's of Alnwick, which is suitable for large loch trout, seatrout and salmon. Many successful fishers use a light two-handed river salmon rod of 12-13 feet, although these can be heavier and more tiring than necessary.

Great rod length is not usually necessary for effective dapping, especially on western Scottish and Irish lochs where there is usually at least a light breeze. All but the very lightest airs will catch the filaments of the dapping floss worked from a typical loch rod of 10-12 feet, billowing it out as a parabolic series of knotted lengths and carrying it well downwind of the boat. A loch rod of this length allows a good billowing dapping parabola to flow out well downwind, so that the fly can be dapped well ahead of the drifting boat; and this length enables the fisher to exercise all the control that is likely to be needed over the dapped fly and, we hope, the fish that will rise to it and been hooked. If a 10-12 foot loch rod can readily handle the fight of a salmon hooked by conventional wetfly loch techniques from a drifting boat, it can do so with equal ease when dapping is the chosen method.

One of the "musts" in dapping is to use the wind and the rod's angle and reach to keep your dapping floss clear of the water and quite dry at all times. Wet floss means the fine filaments bind together in a soggy string, thereby making it heavy and no longer able to offer a large and light surface area to catch the wind. The floss will of course become thoroughly soaked when a fish is hooked and its diving run takes the floss and the backing monofil well under the water. But once the playing of the fish is finished, the floss should be squeezed as dry as possible in an absorbent cloth, in paper tissues or a chamois leather to remove all excess water, and a thorough spraying with water-repellent silicone should do the rest, enabling the floss to be fluffed out into action again. The modern synthetic flosses tend to be naturally fairly water repellent, and if they are kept dressed with a spray-on preparation they should keep generally dry and fluffy. But the skilful dapping angler will ensure that he never allows the floss to dip into the water, or to lie on it and become submerged, while he is fishing. To do this would be to deprive the dapped fly of the life that only the wind's action on the freely blowing floss can impart, and a length of bulky and brightly coloured floss flying idly in the water is also calculated to frighten every fish in sight.

For a dapping reel all that is required is a free-running centrepin model, and if you choose to use a long carbon rod or an even longer telescopic fibreglass rod (they run up to 17 feet) it will be an advantage if your reel is on the heavy side. This helps to balance a long and heavy rod which is held fairly upright during most dapping sessions, and many enthusiasts use an old style salmon fly reel or even a sea-fisher's centrepin reel. Filled with plenty of monofilament line this will not only give a good balancing weight, but also allow a fairly speedy retrieve with a large diameter spool. Some dappers also use fixed-spool reels, which can hold plenty of monofil plus the short terminal length of blow-line, and combine an adjustable drag with speed line retrieval if required.

On a loch-style fly rod in the range 10-12 feet my preference is for one of the geared fly reels such as the Shakespeare Speedex or the Gearfly. These can hold 200 yards or more of monofil, and the geared mechanism allows a very fast rate of line recovery when necessary. Such a reel, when loaded with monofil for dapping, can also double as an excellent trolling reel if you decide to trail a Devon, a toby or some other type of trolling lure – attached, of course, to a leader a good deal finer than the main 20-30lb monofil line. Contrary to some opinions, it is not essential to use either a multiplier or a fixed spool reel to troll effectively from a boat, and these geared fly reels are capable of playing a salmon off the reel with considerable authority and sensitivity.

Any of these setups is fine for a "dedicated" dapping reel, to be kept principally for that purpose, but a very effective ad hoc system can be set up quickly by attaching a length of dapping floss to the end of a normal flyline, whether floating or sinking type. It is a simple matter to keep a spool of dapping floss, or one or two ready cut and knotted lengths of blow-line, in your tackle bag, and to add this to the end of a conventional flyline when you wish to change to dapping tactics.

Dapping flies, as popularly portrayed, tend to look like miniature bottle brushes or something you might use to scrub out the barrels of a shotgun. In fact, their heavily palmered hackles and prominent moustache-like tufts of hair serve three main purposes – to catch the breeze, to present a large area of light and buoyant material to the surface of the water, and to create a prominent and enticing silhouette to any fish watching from below. Most dapping flies for seatrout and salmon are tied on long shanked single hooks from size 10 up to size 6 and sometimes even size 4. Further refinements can be added in the form of one or additional small treble hooks – "flying trebles" – which can reduce the incidence of mis-takes when a fish rises clumsily or takes short, and also add weight to the fly, which can be useful in a stiff breeze when a lighter fly might be whipped about too quickly and unpredictably by the wind.

Dapping patterns tend all to be based upon a foundation of heavy palmering along the whole length of the main hook shank, and hackles of all colours can be encouraged from black and dark brown to pale grey and white. Particular success seems to go to the multi-coloured and bi-visible dressings, which divide the mini bottle brush into segments of darker and lighter material, offering a subtly changing silhouette and differing degrees of translucency when viewed against the light. So long as they are used sparingly, modern synthetic materials such as strands of reflective hair and opalescent filaments can further enhance the allure of these large, bobbing, dancing flies.

I know of two consistently successful loch salmon flyfishers who have largely abandoned the traditional hairy dapping patterns and fare well with very large Muddler Minnow-type flies, in a variety of colours, and also use the Grey Wulff and Royal Wulff patterns dressed on size 10 and 8 hooks in an especially bushy style, with very prominent "horns" protruding at the front.

The choice of dapping fly colour tends to depend on the prevailing light conditions, and the old rule of thumb that dictates "dull day, dark fly – bright day, bright fly" is helpful here. But ring the changes if one colour fails to get a response from the fish. Fly size is largely dictated by the wind and the wave size. A good dapping day with a nice tripping wave and a steady breeze may indicate a size 8 fly, while a stiff wind and rolling surge may mean a move up to size 6 or even larger. In light airs and barely rippling water a size 10 or 12 may be quite sufficient.

A further refinement of the dapping technique is to place the main dapping pattern on a dropper and add a second fly, attached to the leader some 9-18 inches below the surface fly. For this a more typical wet fly or nymph pattern is usually chosen. This can be used as a helpful anchor in a strong or blustery wind, especially if a weighted pattern is used, and this assists greatly in keeping a measure of controlled and gentle tension on the leader while the upper bob-fly is free to trickle and skip about on the surface on its dropper. And even in calm conditions, a small wet fly or nymph pattern fishing just below the surface may take fish which have initially been lured up to inspect the antics of the larger surface fly, just as happens when a tripping bob-fly is used on top of a team of wet flies in traditional loch style short-line fishing. A wide range of proven loch and river patterns can be used, on single and double hooks,

For dapping in a light ripple with the smaller sizes of flies it may be necessary to drop down to a main leader and dropper line of 8 or 6lbs b.s., perhaps with the smaller point fly or an even lighter tippet. This light leader tackle calls for delicacy in playing a fish, of course, but should still be capable of subduing seatrout, grilse and summer salmon quite adequately.

When fishing Irish and Scottish lochs, my list of preferences for a second fly are headed by the Black Pennell, the Invicta and the Green Peter, in sizes from 8 down to 12 and sometimes even 14, depending on the conditions. The Black Pennell will tend to be used on duller days, the Invicta in brighter conditions, and the Green Peter at almost any time. These are all proven loch patterns, and can be dressed on single or double hooks, with or without the addition of lead foil for extra weight in a big blow and a lively wave.

It is easy to learn to dap badly, and not much more difficult to learn to dap competently. Within five or ten minutes any tyro or even a reluctant girlfriend or spouse who has never before handled any fishing rod can learn to keep a buoyant fly bobbing and tripping over the waves, waves which are the product of that same breeze which makes dapping possible. But the advanced dapper will be able to work his fly – or two flies – through a wide arc of up to 90 degrees, or much more if he is the only one fishing, especially is there is a gillie to take over the management of the boat. Tripping a fly on the water ahead of the boat downwind can be varied by periods of moving the fly across the wind. While a fluffy fly trundling down the wind may be little more animated than a tuft of dandelion seeds, the impression of an insect-like silhouette making its apparently difficult way across or against the wind is very likelike, suggestive of a living, struggling insect skating or flying with an effort across the water's surface.

Try to avoid boredom and lapsed concentration when dapping, if good opportunities are not to be lost. The lively salmon and grilse of late summer require sharp wits and a ready but controlled response if a swirling rise is to be followed by a well bent rod, a wet net and a silvery fish in the boat. It is just as important to remain alert and to concentrate on the working of that dipping, tripping fly on the waves as it is to watch your fly and work it carefully across a river pool. To fall into mere mechanical dapping is to fish like an automaton, and is unlikely to be successful. But a ready alertness should certainly not mean that you snatch to tighten quickly on a salmon which takes your dap. Every fish which comes up to a dap needs to be given time to turn over and downwards with the fly in its mouth before tension is applied on the line, which with luck will then draw the hook into the angle of the jaws, that most secure and desirable of hook-holds. Incredibly, a full 5-7 seconds is sometimes reckoned to be right for biggish trout on some big Irish stillwaters, and although salmon do not need such a very restrained response it still pays dividends to allow a definite pause until the rising fish has turned over fully, taken the fly into its mouth and turned downwards again. Then a firm tightening of the line should pull the fly into the jaws' scissors.

If the fish takes your second, subsurface fly rather different responses are called for. You are likely to see a much less dramatic rise than if the fish had come right up to your bob-fly, and in a sizeable wave you may see little or nothing until the tug of the fish's take signals that something has happened. Then you should tighten firmly and promptly, but not abruptly, and the chances are that you will discover the fish has taken the fly with a turning movement and has immediately hooked itself in the scissors as you felt the take.

A word of caution is necessary when dapping with a powerful rod, especially a river salmon rod or one of the long telescopic dapping models. These are doughty rods, of considerable power, and can subdue even a big fish in short order. But they can also place excessive and insensitive pressure on the fly's hook-hold, and on a light leader such as you may use in calm, bright conditions. No-one wants to lose a good fish by having the hook tear out or the leader snap under excessive strain, so use the big rods with care.

A net is the only suitable method of getting a beaten salmon into the boat. Although tailing is possible, with great care, any attempt to do so will

A telescopic dapping rod and a selection of flies in boxes, for loch salmon and grilse.

involve one of the boat's occupants leaning dangerously far over the side, and there is too high a risk of taking a tumble or even capsizing the boat. A tailer may perhaps secure a salmon for you, but will usually fail to hold a grilse or a seatrout, and the handles of most models are not long enough for easy use from a boat in any case. A gaff is out for the same reason, as well as for its other disadvantages. The only worthwhile method is to ensure that the boat carries a good net, preferably with a handle not less than 60 inches long, with a diameter of at least 30 inches, and a net depth of 36 inches. A dry net tends to float, and even a wetted net may not sink enough for comfort, so it is worth having a weight in the bottom of the net bag to sink it quickly. The old gillie's trick is to keep in the toe of the net a rounded stone the size and weight of a small cobblestone. Another useful trick is to attach to the toe of the net a few rings of lead cut from a discarded piece of lead water-piping.

A beaten fish should be drawn close to the boat and over the already sunken net, which is then lifted quickly and firmly to bring the fish out of the water and swing it into the boat. No attempt should be made to scoop or spoon a fish out with the net. It may trigger a last-minute panic by the fish, and there is a very good chance you will lose it. And once it is in the boat, a salmon should be held firmly with one hand grasping it across the shoulders, while the other administers the last rites with the priest. Do not delay this, or allow a dying salmon to thrash about in the boat. Even a small fish is powerful enough to thrash itself up off the boards and collapse on top of a valuable carbon rod, snapping it like a twig or, perhaps worse, leaving it apparently unharmed but fatally weakened. Then it may shatter without warning sometime later as you are casting or playing a fish.

Once safely dealt with, a salmon deserves to be kept in good condition. A long day in a boat will dessicate its skin and ruin its appearance, especially if there is a warm sun beating down on it. Keep all fish in a thoroughly damp fish bass, preferably of woven rush or hessian and not the modern synthetic types, or hang them in the water by looping the handles of your bass over the boat's upwind rowlock or thole pin – provided the handles are sound, of course.

Chapter 16   Kelts, Catch-and-release, and Conservation

A kelt is a salmon or grilse (and the term is sometimes also applied to a seatrout) which has spawned and then survived in the river through the late winter. In appearance and in its behaviour after it has been hooked it is very different from a fresh fish or an imminent spawner, and there should be no real excuse for mistaking a kelt for a keepable fish. The typical fullness of body of the fresh-run salmon has been replaced by a lank and heavy-headed slenderness, the vent is prominent and raw in appearance, the fins are frayed and tattered, and the gills are invariably heavily infested with fresh-water maggots. The glorious silver of its spring colour, or the richness of its pre-spawning livery, has been replaced by an unpleasantly harsh and bright metallic sheen. It probably weighs less than half its weight when it originally re-entered the river, and it may attack a fly or any other lure with ravenous lack of discrimination. Its suppressed feeding urge has recovered, and with a bit of luck it will revive, dropping back downstream and then out to sea, eventually to resume the full bodied muscularity of an adult salmon and perhaps to make a second or even a third spawning run back to the nursery streams of its infancy and first mating.

Kelts are an occupational hazard for the spring salmon fisher, and their readiness to take a fly or a spinner means that many are hooked unintentionally. Apart from the fact that it is illegal to keep or kill spent or unclean salmon, it is a wise procedure to bring a kelt to the net as quickly as possible, to unhook it carefully, and to return it to the water gently. With luck it may still recover and return again to the river another time.

The only time it should be necessary to dispatch a kelt is if it has been so badly hooked that there is no hope of extracting the hooks without first killing the fish, or if there is profuse bleeding from its mouth or tongue after the hooks have been taken out. Then it is only humane to use the priest, and you can probably find a cat which will be happy enough to dine off the carcase.

When returning an undamaged kelt to the river, the fish should be held with one hand grasping it securely in the tailing position, with fingers and thumb around the wrist of the tail, while the other hand is cupped under the fish's belly and supports most of its weight. It should be supported gently in the water, its head pointed upstream to allow the current to flow through its gills, and given time to resume normal breathing functions and to recover its balance. If this is successful, the limp body will gradually recover strength and energy, eventually wresting itself away from your gentle grasp and off to freedom.

Wish it well as it goes. It has already survived untold hundreds of miles of hazardous sea life, run the gauntlets of seals, nets and rod-fishers, and endured the debilitating rigours of mating and spawning. It remains weak and vulnerable until it is well out to sea again, where the rich feeding may restore it to full vitality again.

Catch-and-release and Conservation
The principle of catch-and-release involves a fish being hooked and played in the normal way, and brought to the net, if all goes well, whereupon the (usually barbless) hook is removed, and the fish, having perhaps been photographed and weighed, is carefully returned to the water, the fisher doing his best to restore its equilibrium by steadying it in the current and then allowing it to swim off to freedom. The object of catch-and-release is to allow rod-and-line anglers to enjoy all the challenges of finding, enticing, hooking and playing a fish, without the catching culminating in the fish's death. Instead, it is returned to the water in the hope that it will go on to spawn and thereby to make a contribution to the future of its species in those waters.

Despite the apparent logic of that straightforward-looking argument, catch-and-release is a vexatious and controversial issue among British game anglers, although it is widely accepted by anglers in North America, and has of course been practised for generations by British coarse-fishers. In Britain it is standard practice for coarse fish to be retained alive in the confines of a keep-net until the day's fishing or the competition is over, when the total catch is weighed and then liberated.

Among freshwater game fishers, a vocal pro-c&r lobby argues that the catching of a wild salmon or trout is a sufficient end in itself, and that it is both unnecessary and destructive to kill and keep every fish caught – or, indeed, any fish at all, since sport not sustenance is the object of game fishing in the developed western nations. This argument is especially urged on waters where wild and natural salmon stocks have seriously declined, and where rod fishing may be perceived as an unnecessary additional pressure on depleted salmon numbers. Better for conservation, they argue, that fish should be returned alive and as carefully as possible, in the expectation that they will breed and help perpetuate the species' abundance in the wild, not least for the satisfaction of future generations of fishers.

On the face of it, that may seem to be a commendable policy, but it only has value if the released fish have a realistic chance of going on to fulfil their freshwater destiny, by spawing successfully. But will a salmon that has been played on rod and line, and brought to the net, be able to recover and survive in a fit state to do this?

A fresh springer, caught in the full vigour of its prime state in March or April, has to survive to a further seven or more months of life in the river system before it is time to pair off and spawn, and during that long interval it will eat nothing, relying on its reserves of condition acquired from the rich feeding it has enjoyed at sea. A fresh salmon fights with every ounce of its considerable energy, and will not come to the net until it is thoroughly beaten. Is it always realistic to expect such a fish to revive and have a good chance of surviving until it spawns the following winter? And what if it does recover from that first catching and releasing, only to fall victim to another angler's fly a few weeks or months later, to be released a second time? Is the re-caught fish still a truly "wild" salmon, or has it already forfeited that description through being caught and returned? Will its second fight be worthy of a salmon, and, more importantly, may not that second struggle exhaust it utterly and bring about its death before it can spawn? Then it will have failed either to reproduce its kind or to provide a fine meal at the supper table, and its death will have been largely in vain, apart from the two relatively brief periods of personal excitement it provided for the two fishers who successively caught and released it. Even if a salmon is only caught once, the sporting angler who unhooks and returns such a fish, or the fishery proprietor who requires his Rods to do so, must face up to the serious questions, both practical and ethical, that are raised by the act of catch-and-release.

First, does c&r make a significant contribution to the conservation of the species? Scientific research may yield the answer, in time. However, it seems unreasonable on elementary ecological grounds to expect that a policy of catch-and-release will contribute to effective conservation unless the spawning and nursery habitats of the salmon within the river are good, and complemented by favourable conditions at sea, with ample food for fast growth to maturity, and a worthwhile measure of protection from disease, excessive predation, and human over-exploitation. There is little if any evidence to indicate that legitimate rod-fishing is jeopardising the wild salmon populations of any catchment in the British Isles, but all too many reasons to believe that wild salmon numbers have dwindled owing to pollution, degradation of their freshwater habitat, and grossly excessive exploitation by netting, on the high seas, offshore and close to river estuaries. To permit these gross abuses to continue and pretend that catch-and-release can make a worthwhile contribution to salmon conservation is simply absurd.

Secondly, is c&r a sporting and ethically acceptable practice for anglers? By their nature, ethical questions cannot be answered by adopting the rigorously objective methods of the scientist. What is ethically right, which in fishing means what is sporting and fair to the fish, can only be determined by reference to some moral code, and the British game fishing press has seen a good deal of public wrangling over the ethics of c&r since the 1980s, in the course of which two substantial bodies of opinion have emerged, each adhering to quite distinct codes of angling ethics.

The proponents of c&r argue that what matters to the sporting fisherman is the challenge of luring, hooking and playing a fish, and that its death is unnecessary, since today's sporting fishermen have no need to rely for food on what they catch. They contend that species conservation is best served by returning all uninjured fish to the water.

Opponents of c&r take the view that the humane despatching of the fish with a priest is an essential part of catching game fish with rod and line, and believe that to go fishing with the intention of catching and releasing a fish, perhaps more than once, is fundamentally to change its status from a worthy wild quarry to a mere fisherman's plaything, an object prized only for the gratification we get from deceiving, hooking and playing it.

Powerful and sincere arguments exist on both sides, and any thoughtful game fisher will give these issues the long and careful consideration they deserve. Each individual's conscience is, after all, the yardstick by which such ethical decisions are ultimately made. My own view, after a great deal of thought, is to oppose blanket policies of catch-and-release. I feel that salmon, and all other fish, deserve better than to be played hard and subjected to the stresses of being caught, only to be returned and perhaps caught again. Furthermore, I dislike the philosophy of angling which involves fishing hard, sometimes catching fish after fish, only for all of them to be returned. This seems to me to be gratuitously stressful to the individual fish involved, and demeaning to the species as a whole, which ceases to be a respected wild quarry for the hunter – and everyone who fishes for wild fish is, in truth, a hunter – and becomes no more than a source of amusement to the angler. That, I feel, cannot be good sportsmanship. Instead it becomes competitive and exploitative.

However, I have no such reservations about the traditional procedures whereby certain specific types of salmon – and trout and seatrout – are released alive. For generations this has been standard practice when hen fish heavy with eggs are caught towards the end of the season, and also when spent post-spawners – kelts – are caught, and also baggots, salmon which are heavy with roe but have failed to spawn for some reason. The law requires us to return kelts and baggots, which have long been deemed "unclean fish", and conventional sporting procedure is to put back all gravid hens in autumn, unless (and this is the only exception) they happen to have been so badly damaged as to have no realistic prospect of surviving to spawn. In this, the game fisher is guided not only by the law and local regulations regarding the official open and closed seasons, but also by his personal judgement of the fish in question. The offence of killing "unseasonable fish" can still occur even if the close season has not yet begun, as was forcefully underlined by a notable court judgment in Scotland in 1992. Heavily gravid hen salmon must always be returned to the water, and the only acceptable defence for killing such a fish is that it has been so badly injured by the hook or some other means that it must be despatched.

But by returning autumn hen fish, are we not being inconsistent, and actually practicing a limited form of c&r? Not so. No-one sets out with the *intention* of catching gravid hen fish, whereas, by definition, the c&r devotee sets out to catch and release all his fish, and that I find objectionable. Once an angler has convinced himself that fish can be caught and released with impunity, he is likely to go on doing it. This philosophy can lead to unrestrained fishing pressure, which is unjustifiable. Far better, I believe, to exercise self-restraint, and to catch and keep only a reasonable number of well-grown, clean and seasonable fish.

In the matter of sporting ethics, our intentions are what really matter. We do not intend to catch fish that are heavy with roe and in advanced spawning livery, nor to catch parr and undersized fish, nor to catch a trout in the close season when it happens to take a fly that we are legitimately fishing for grayling. In all these instances we return the fish as carefully as we can, for it was never our intention to catch them in the first place.

But our intentions must be realistic and rational, too. There will be times when the conditions make it extremely probable that what we catch will be mainly undersized or unseasonable fish, and then we have to make an individual decision about whether we should cast a line or not. For instance, it would be unrealistic to claim that you intend to catch only fresh-run fish in an autumn river that is self-evidently full of dark coloured and gravid fish, with no indications of a recent run of fresh salmon. In making this assessment the flyfisherman is at a disadvantage compared to, for example, the game shooter. When an undersized pheasant is flushed, or a black grouse flies within shot on The Twelfth when only red grouse are in season, the discriminating shooter can see the situation and hold his fire, letting the bird pass unscathed. The flyfisher, however, is unlikely to be aware of anything until his fly is taken, and then can only make an informed guess as to its species, size and condition until, as the fight proceeds, he eventually gets a good clear look at the fish. Then, if he sees that it is a kelt or a gravid fish, he can play it accordingly, allowing every opportunity for the hook-hold to fail, or bringing it in as quickly as possible and releasing it with the minimum of handling.

The pleasure of catching exciting, wild game fish is an indulgence best enjoyed in moderation, like most pleasures. Self-discipline in fishing is as important as self-restraint in any other activity. Enough is as good as a feast, especially when over-indulgence means you may be putting a fishery and the future of its salmon in jeopardy. Even worse, perhaps, overdoing it may call into question the good name of game fishing in general, and thus play into the hands of those who would like to see all sporting fishing with rod and line banned. No sportsman will do anything that would offer such a hostage to fortune, and the self-discipline of the ethical sportsman will always be preferable to the imposition of formal laws and regulations. Rigid pronouncements and edicts about field sports are a two-edged sword. To create a statutory catch-limit may not simply outlaw the taking of excessive baskets of fish; it may also unintentionally encourage fishers to press hard to achieve that limit. "Limit the catch, not catch the limit" is one of the wisest adages of fishing – and of all field sports – in the late 20th century.

By the same token, we should think carefully about what we would and should do if – and it is a very big 'if' – we ever had one of those extraordinary days when one or two rods are likely to make a very big killing. It can still happen – though very seldom compared with the days of abundant fish and low angling pressures – that a combination of salmon numbers, water height and flow, barometric pressure, and other factors at which perhaps we can still only guess, creates a situation in which almost every cast will bring a take. Some Victorian and Edwardian bonanza catches have been quite well documented, on waters such as the Grimersta in Lewis, the River Moy in Ireland and the Tay and the Tweed where single Rods have caught three or four dozen fish in a day, and two Rods sharing a beat have topped the 100 mark in a single day's fishing. It still occasionally happens, although it is significant that such rare events are now seldom publicised by those involved. The modern angler is aware of pressures of public opinion and of censure motivated by a concern for conservation that simply did not apply in our grandfather's day. No-one wants to overdo it – or, let's be honest, no-one wants to be *seen* to overdo it, for the sin of being found out often weighs more heavily on the conscience than the fact of having done the deed.

So what would you – what would I? – do, if we each had, say, six salmon on the grass in the first two hours, with perhaps eight or ten more hours of prime fishing time still in hand? I like to think that I would have the strength of will to stop and reel in, because I know that would be the right, the sporting thing to do. But probably none of us really knows what we would do, until the occasion arises.

Bibliography

1. The Salmon's Natural History and Conservation:

Ade, Robin *A Trout and Salmon Handbook* 1989
Jenkins, D. & W.M. Shearer *The Status of the Atlantic Salmon in Scotland* 1986
Mills, Derek *Salmon & Trout: A Resource, its Ecology, Conservation and
   Management* 1971
Mills, Derek *The Ecology and Management of Atlantic Salmon* 1989
Netboy, Anthony *The Atlantic Salmon: A Vanishing Species?* 1968
Netboy, Anthony *The Salmon: Their Fight for Survival* 1973
Netboy, Anthony *Salmon: The World's Most Harassed Fish* 1980
Went, A.E.J. (edit.) *The Atlantic Salmon: Its Future* 1980

2. National and Regional Guides for Salmon Fishers:

Ashley Cooper, John *The Great Salmon Rivers of Scotland* 1980
Little, Crawford *The Great Salmon Beats* 1989
Little, Crawford *Salmon and Sea Trout Fisheries of Scotland* 1990
McKelvie, Colin *A Gamefisher in Ireland* 1989
O'Reilly, Peter *The Trout and Salmon Loughs of Ireland* 1992
O'Reilly, Peter *The Trout and Salmon Rivers of Ireland* 1993

3. Guides to Salmon Flies and Patterns:

Buckland, John & Arthur Oglesby *A Guide to Salmon Flies* 1990
Mackenzie-Philps, Peter *Successful Modern Salmon Flies* 1989
Malone, E.J. *Irish Trout & Salmon Flies* 1984
Rice, Freddie *Flytying Illustrated: Salmon & Seatrout Patterns* 1990
Waltham, James *Classic Salmon Flies: The Francis Francis Collection* 1983

4. Guides to Fly Casting:

Falkus, Hugh *Spey Casting: A New Technique* 1994
Mackenzie-Philps, Peter *Flycasting Handbook* 1991

5. Classic and Recent Guides to Flyfishing for Salmon:

Anderson, Gary *The Atlantic Salmon: Fact and Fantasy* 1990
Chaytor, A.H. *Letters to a Salmon Fisher's Sons* 1910
Falkus, Hugh *Salmon Fishing: A Practical Guide* 1984
Graesser, Neil *Advanced Salmon Fishing* 1987
Graesser, Neil *Salmon* 1991
Grant, Francis T. *Salmon Flyfishing: The Dynamics Approach* 1993
Green, Philip *New Angles on Salmon Fishing* 1984
Knowles, Derek *Salmon on a Dry Fly* 1987

Lapsley, Peter (edit.) *The Complete Flyfisher* 1990
Little, Crawford *Success With Salmon* 1988
Little, Crawford *The Salmon Fisherman's Year* 1990
Oglesby, Arthur *Salmon* 1971, rev. 1983
Oglesby, Arthur *Flyfishing for Salmon and Sea Trout* 1986
"Scott, Jock" *Greased-Line Fishing for Salmon* 1935
Spencer, Stanley *Fishing the Wilder Shores* 1991
Sutherland, Douglas *The Salmon Book* 1982
Waddington, Richard *Waddington on Salmon Fishing* 1981
Wrangles, Alan (edit.) *Salmon and Sea Trout Fishing* 1989
Wulff, Lee *The Atlantic Salmon* 1983

Index